200 meals for two

200 meals for two

hamlyn **all color**

Louise Blair

An Hachette UK Company
www.hachette.co.uk

First published in Great Britain in 2010 by Hamlyn,
a division of Octopus Publishing Group Ltd
2–4 Heron Quays, London E14 4JP
www.octopusbooksusa.com

Copyright © Octopus Publishing Group Ltd 2010

Distributed in the U.S. and Canada by
Octopus Books USA:
c/o Hachette Book Group USA
237 Park Avenue
New York, NY 10017

Some of the recipes in this book have previously
appeared in other books published by Hamlyn.

ISBN: 978-0-600-62017-4

A CIP catalog record for this book is available
from the Library of Congress

Printed and bound in China

1 2 3 4 5 6 7 8 9 10

Standard level spoon measurements are used in all recipes.

Ovens should be preheated to the specified temperature—if
using a fan-assisted oven, follow the manufacturer's
instructions for adjusting the time and the temperature.

Fresh herbs should be used unless otherwise stated.

Medium eggs should be used unless otherwise stated.

The Food and Drug Administration advises that eggs
should not be consumed raw. This book contains
some dishes made with raw or lightly cooked eggs. It
is prudent for vulnerable people such as pregnant and
nursing mothers, invalids, the elderly, babies, and young
children to avoid uncooked or lightly cooked dishes made
with eggs. Once prepared, these dishes should be kept
refrigerated and used promptly.

This book includes dishes made with nuts and nut
derivatives. It is advisable for those with known allergic
reactions to nuts and nut derivatives and those who
may be potentially vulnerable to these allergies to avoid
dishes made with nuts and nut oils. It is also prudent
to check the labels of pre-prepared ingredients for the
possible inclusion of nut derivatives.

contents

introduction

introduction

Most cookery books give recipes that are designed for four people, sometimes more, so when you are cooking for just two people what should you do?

Of course, some recipes are fairly easy to scale down by cutting ingredients in half, and many work well when you do this. But what do you do when it comes to halving ingredients such as a single egg or small amounts of herbs and spices? And what about cooking times? Should you halve them or leave them as for the original quantities of ingredients? The recipes in this book remove any guesswork and fiddly calculations, giving you plenty of delicious meals, from simple snacks to dishes for special occasions, all of which can easily be doubled or scaled up even more for over four diners.

With just a little thought and planning, cooking for just two people can become a pleasure, rather than a chore. Don't make things unnecessarily difficult for yourself. Choose ingredients that are easy to come by and select recipes that are straightforward and quick to make and that are, above all, taste delicious.

We are all aware of the healthy eating guidelines that the government and, increasingly, supermarkets are urging us to follow—though we should never forget that occasionally a little of what you fancy won't do any harm. For day-to-day nutrition and good health, however, we should bear the following in mind and try to eat:

• More fruit and vegetables: our aim should be at least five portions a day. Try drinking a glass of fruit juice with breakfast and add some chopped fresh fruit to your cereal, and you'll be off to a great start.

• More starchy foods, such as rice, bread, pasta, and potatoes. Carbohydrates should make up the biggest portion of your meal, followed by vegetables and protein. Slow-releasing, ("good") carbs, help to fill you up and to keep your energy levels constant throughout the day. Choose wholegrain varieties, wherever possible, as these contain more goodness.

• Less fat, salt, and sugar. You should always check the labels on canned and packaged foods, but it's easy to overlook this when you're in a hurry. Obviously, cooking from scratch is the best way to ensure minimal salt and sugar content and be sparing about adding salt during cooking. Trimming excess fat from meat and changing to lower-fat dairy products will also help to reduce your fat intake.

• Some protein-rich foods, such as meat, eggs, legumes, and fish: the recommendation is that we eat at least two portions of fish or shellfish each week, and one of these should be an oily fish, which is high in essential omega-3 fatty acid.

Healthy eating is also about using healthy cooking techniques and these can really help you to cut down on your fat intake, as well as maximize the nutritional value of your food. It might be worth investing in a steamer. They aren't very expensive and can be used for cooking all your vegetables, as well as some meat and fish. When you boil vegetables, much of the vitamin content is lost in the cooking liquid, whereas steaming retains it in the food. Another quick change is to grill or broil food instead of frying. Fish and meat just need a very light brush of oil before being placed on the grill or under the broiler.

menu planning

Take some time to prepare a weekly menu plan. This doesn't have to be set in stone, of course, and if your plans change it shouldn't be a problem to re-jig the menu and pop some things in the freezer for another week.

Sensible planning means that if you want a roast meal then next day you use the leftover meat in a stir-fry or for a salad lunch. Broccoli cooked to accompany roast dinner one day could be used in Sausage and Broccoli Pasta (see pages 148–9) later in the week.

Where appropriate, double up quantities so that you can freeze individual portions to enjoy a couple of weeks later.

Remember to use your oven wisely: if you are making a casserole, roast potatoes at the same time or bake a dessert. This is a great way of saving energy and money.

Spend time writing a list for your weekly shop; you can keep these lists in a file or on your computer so that when you next plan a week with similar meals you have a list ready. Try to make the most of special offers if you can—extra meat and fish can be divided into portions for one and two and frozen for later use. A shopping list will help to prevent you from falling into the trap of buying things that you won't actually use.

Try to plan recipes that make the most of seasonal ingredients. Not only are vegetables and fruit cheaper when they are in season, but they often have a far better flavor. Also look out for locally produced goods that will be both fresh and flavorsome and will also help to keep down food miles. If you are lucky enough to have a local farmer's market or a street market near you, make the time to look around for really fresh and well-flavored produce. Good-quality meat and fish then needs little adornment beyond a selection of steamed vegetables and perhaps some herb-flavored butter (see pages 156–7)—nothing could be tastier or simpler.

pantry essentials

You will soon find that there are some ingredients that you use every week and that you need to keep in stock.

• **Oils:** buy good-quality olive oil, which as well as being beneficial to your health is also a great staple for sauces, dressings, and marinades. You will also need a vegetable or sunflower oil for cooking.

• **Mustards:** Dijon, wholegrain, and English mustard will give depth of flavor to sauces and a kick to dressings and, of course, they can be used as an accompaniment to meats or in a sandwich.

• **Pasta:** perfect with a simple sauce for quick suppers; remember that different shapes suit different dishes. It's often easier to stick to one or two of your favorite shapes so that you aren't left with half-used packages, each containing not quite enough for a meal.

• **Rice:** as with pastas there are several types to choose from, but basmati and risotto rices are always useful.

• **Sundried tomatoes:** chop these and add them to salads or pasta dishes.

• **Tomato paste:** use tomato paste or passata in sauces for pasta dishes, such as Bolognese. Keep jars in the refrigerator with the date you opened them written on so you don't forget.

• **Canned beans:** a great stand-by, canned beans—cannellini, kidney, and cranberry beans, for example—don't need the long soaking and cooking of the dried equivalent, and they can be added to salads, soups, and stews for vegetarians, giving a wonderful texture and taste. See, for example, Bean soup with guacamole (pages 64–5) and Italian bean & artichoke salad (pages 102–3).

• **Pine nuts:** quickly toasted, they are delicious additions to pastas and salads.

• **Sauces:** bottles of light and dark soy sauce and fish sauce (nam pla) are essential if you enjoy Eastern dishes of any kind.

• **Herbs and spices:** of course, fresh herbs have the best flavors, but not everyone has

access to a herb garden or has the space to keep more than a few essentials growing on a windowsill. Packs or little jars of dried herbs, such as thyme, oregano, and marjoram, and spices, such as chili powder, garam masala, cumin, coriander, and peppercorns, are useful, but remember to use them up because they lose their characteristic flavors over time.

• **Curry paste:** the ideal pantry ingredient, a good-quality ready-made curry paste will allow you to stir-fry some vegetables with leftover meat or shrimp. Simply stir in some coconut milk and serve with rice for a delicious and speedy supper.

refrigerator essentials

Your weekly shopping list will almost certainly include some, if not all, of the following:

• **Cheese:** a well-flavored cheddar cheese can be used for quick snacks, sandwiches, and for grating into salads, while feta cheese can be crumbled into pasta dishes or used in salads. Parmesan cheese is not only essential for pasta and risottos but is also used in pesto and sauces.

• **Bacon:** chopped and cooked with a little garlic and tossed through pasta with a little light cream and some Parmesan cheese gives you a carbonara in minutes.

• **Fresh pasta and sauces:** although it is quick and easy to cook your own pasta and sauce, the ready-made packages can be prepared in minutes and are a good standby,

especially if you have some fresh Parmesan to grate over them.

• **Free-range eggs:** omelets and frittatas are perfect meals for two people. Quick and easy to prepare and cook, they are the ideal way of using up leftover vegetables at the end of the week.

using your freezer

Before you put anything in your freezer make sure it's clearly labeled, and don't forget to include the date, so you know when it should be used by—things don't last forever, even in the freezer.

If you have time to cook in bulk, stock up your freezer to save yourself time and money. Shepherd's pies, lasagnas, Bolognese sauce, chili con carne, stews and casseroles, and even portions of mashed potato all freeze well, and these dishes can be complete life-savers when the cabinets are bare or you have unexpected visitors.

Frozen fruits and vegetables are always useful—frozen spinach, for example, can be quickly thawed and tossed through cooked pasta with a little cream, Parmesan cheese, and a few toasted pine nuts. Frozen fruits can be popped into a blender with some fruit juice and yogurt to make an instant and filling smoothie. Freezing is also a great way to make the most of seasonal fruit and vegetables. Berries freeze particularly well and can be bought or picked when in abundance and then frozen for use during the winter months. The best way to freeze berries is to spread them in a single layer on a baking sheet and then pop them in the freezer. Once they're solid you can transfer them into labeled bags. That way, they won't all freeze together in lumps and you'll be able to take out just a handful when you need them.

basic recipes

Get really organized by having some pesto and homemade stock on standby.

homemade pesto

Although you can buy ready-made pesto in supermarkets and delicatessens, it is easy and quick to make at home. In a food processor or blender process together ½ garlic clove, 2 large handfuls of fresh basil, a handful of toasted pine nuts, 2 tablespoons grated Parmesan cheese, and 6 tablespoons olive oil. Season to taste with salt and pepper. This will keep in a screw-top jar in the

can use leftover meat carcasses for chicken or beef stocks. Add some chopped carrots and onions to water. Add flavorings, such as peppercorns, bouquet garni, bay leaves, and herbs, then bring to a boil and simmer for at least 1 hour. Allow to cool, then strain. The cooled stock can be frozen in portions and used as needed. See page 146 for a full version of a chicken stock recipe.

If making your own stock seems like too much effort or you really don't have the time, use one of the liquid stocks that are now available in supermarkets. Look out, too, for ready-made marinades in the herbs and spices sections of delicatessens and supermarkets and use them to add flavor to meat and fish before cooking.

refrigerator for 3–4 days. Toss the pesto through pasta or spread it over ciabatta or toast and top with vine-ripened tomatoes and torn mozzarella. Alternatively, combine it with a little mayonnaise (see pages 70–71) or sour cream, and stir through cooked new potatoes and griddled chicken or serve it with salad.

good-quality stock

Homemade stock is the basis of many recipes, and although you can buy cubes and powders to make up with water, a well-flavored homemade stock will make a real difference to your cooking. There is a recipe for vegetable stock on pages 94–5, but you

brunch

blueberry french toasts

Serves **2**
Preparation time **5 minutes**
Cooking time **5 minutes**

2 **eggs**, beaten
6 tablespoons **light cream** or
  milk
¼ teaspoon **ground
  cinnamon**
2 **brioches**, cut in half
  horizontally
1 tablespoon **unsalted butter**

Blueberry compote
2⅔ cups fresh **blueberries**
1 tablespoon **superfine sugar**

Make the compote. Put the blueberries and half the sugar into a small pan, place over a low heat, and cook for 4–5 minutes until the berries are softened and beginning to ooze their juices. Set aside while you make the toasts.

Beat together the egg, cream or milk, and cinnamon in a shallow bowl. Dip the brioches into the egg mixture and soak well.

Heat the butter in a nonstick skillet, add the brioche, and cook over a medium heat for 3–4 minutes, turning occasionally until browned all over. Serve with the blueberry compote.

For mixed berries with chocolate toasts, make a compote with 2½ cups frozen mixed berries and 1 tablespoon superfine sugar as above. Replace the brioches with 2 pains au chocolat and cook them in the same way as the brioches.

mushroom & pancetta omelet

Serves **2**
Preparation time **15 minutes**
Cooking time **10–12 minutes**

1 tablespoon **olive oil**
6 oz mixed **wild** or **cup mushrooms**, sliced
4 oz **pancetta** or **Canadian bacon**, diced
3 tablespoons **sour cream**
4 teaspoons chopped **thyme**
4 **eggs**, separated
½ teaspoon **Dijon mustard**
1 tablespoon **butter**
salt and **black pepper**

Heat the oil in a large skillet, add the mushrooms and pancetta or bacon, and fry for 5 minutes, stirring frequently, until golden. Stir in the sour cream and thyme, then remove the mixture from the pan and keep hot.

Wash and dry the pan. Beat the egg whites into stiff, moist-looking peaks.

Mix together the egg yolks and mustard and season to taste with salt and pepper. Fold the mixture into the egg whites.

Heat the butter in the skillet, add the egg mixture, and cook over a medium heat for 3–4 minutes until the underside is golden. Quickly transfer the pan to a preheated hot broiler, making sure that the handle is away from the heat, and cook for 2–3 minutes until the top is brown and the center still slightly soft.

Spoon the mushroom and pancetta mixture over the omelet and fold in half. Serve immediately with a mixed salad.

For herb & ricotta omelet, beat 4 egg whites until they form soft peaks. Fold through the egg yolks and add 2 tablespoons chopped mixed herbs and ¼ cup ricotta. Season well with salt and pepper. Heat 2 tablespoons butter in a nonstick skillet. Carefully add the egg mixture and cook for 3 minutes until the underside is golden. Transfer to a preheated broiler as above and cook for 2–3 minutes.

breakfast muesli

Serves **2**
Preparation time **5 minutes**,
  plus soaking

1 cup **jumbo oats**
1 tablespoon **pumpkin seeds**
1 tablespoon **sunflower seeds**
1 tablespoon **sesame seeds**
½ cup ready-to-eat **dried
  apricots,** halved
½ cup **dried cranberries**
1 cup **plain yogurt**

To serve
1 tablespoon **toasted
  almonds**, roughly chopped
2 tablespoons **honey**
milk (optional)

Mix together the oats, seeds, apricots, cranberries, and yogurt. Chill in the refrigerator overnight.

Sprinkle with the almonds and serve the muesli drizzled with the honey and a little milk, if desired.

For tropical muesli, replace the cranberries with ½ cup each of banana chips, dried mango, dried pineapple, and 2 chopped dried figs. Omit the yogurt and serve with milk and a drizzle of honey.

beans & haloumi mushrooms

Serves **2**
Preparation time **10 minutes**
Cooking time **20 minutes**

4 large **portobello
mushrooms**
2 **garlic cloves**, finely
chopped
4 tablespoons chopped
mixed herbs, such as
thyme, rosemary, chives,
and parsley
6 tablespoons **olive oil**
13½ oz can **baked beans**
few drops of **balsamic
vinegar**
8 thin slices of **haloumi
cheese**
black pepper

To serve
2 cups **arugula leaves**
1 **pear**, cored and sliced
¼ cup grated **Parmesan
cheese**

Remove the stems from the mushrooms and place
the caps, gill sides up, in an ovenproof dish. Sprinkle
with half the garlic and herbs and season with black
pepper. Drizzle with half the oil, place in a preheated
oven, 400°F, and roast for 10–15 minutes or until
cooked through.

Mix the beans with a few drops of balsamic vinegar
and heat through gently. Spoon the beans over
the cooked mushrooms and arrange the slices of
haloumi over the beans. Sprinkle with the reserved
garlic and herbs and drizzle with the remaining oil. Put
the dish under a preheated hot broiler and cook for
2–3 minutes or until the haloumi is golden brown.

Divide the dish into individual portions of two
mushrooms each and serve with an arugula, pear, and
Parmesan salad.

For bean & haloumi potato wedges, cut 2 large
potatoes into 8 wedges each and parboil the pieces
for 5 minutes. Drain thoroughly and put the potato
wedges on a baking sheet. Drizzle over 1 tablespoon
olive oil and cook under a preheated hot broiler for
5–7 minutes until golden and tender. Mix 13½ oz can
baked beans with a few drops of balsamic vinegar,
warm through, and spoon over the potato wedges.
Arrange 8 thin slices of haloumi cheese over the
beans and return to the broiler. Cook until bubbling
and golden. Sprinkle with a tablespoon chopped
parsley and serve.

baked eggs with salmon

Serves **2**
Preparation time **5 minutes**
Cooking time **10 minutes**

1 teaspoon **unsalted butter**
4 oz **smoked salmon** or
  smoked trout, cut into bite-
  size pieces
2 large **eggs**
2 tablespoons **heavy cream**
1 tablespoon chopped **herbs**,
  such as chervil and chives
salt and **black pepper**

Grease 2 ramekins, each of ⅔ cup capacity, with butter. Divide the salmon between the ramekins, then break in the eggs.

Mix together the cream and herbs and season to taste with salt and pepper. Pour into the ramekins and place them in a baking pan. Half-fill the pan with boiling water and transfer to a preheated oven, 400°F, for about 10 minutes until the mixture is just set. Serve with triangles of crunchy fresh toast, if desired.

For baked eggs with ham, replace the salmon with 4 oz sliced ham or prosciutto and break the eggs into the ramekins as before. Stir 1 teaspoon wholegrain mustard and 1 tablespoon snipped chives through the cream and add to the eggs. Cook as above until just set.

croque monsieur

Serves **2**
Preparation time **8 minutes**
Cooking time **5 minutes**

4 thick slices of **French
country bread**
2 tablespoons **butter**, melted
¼ cup finely grated **Parmesan
cheese**
2 large slices of **roast ham**
4 oz **Emmental cheese**,
coarsely grated

Use a pastry brush to brush one side of each slice of bread with the melted butter, then sprinkle with the Parmesan.

Place 2 slices of bread on the countertop, with the Parmesan-coated sides face down and top each with a slice of ham and half the Emmental.

Top with the remaining 2 slices of bread, Parmesan-coated sides on the outside, and toast in a sandwich grill for 4–5 minutes or according to the manufacturer's instructions until the bread is golden and crispy and the Emmental is beginning to ooze from the sides. Serve immediately.

For croque madame, make the sandwiches as above and top each one with a fried egg.

eggs benedict with hollandaise

Serves **2**
Preparation time **10 minutes**
Cooking time **5 minutes**

2 large **eggs**
1 **English muffin**, halved
   horizontally and toasted
a little **butter**
4 slices of **prosciutto**
salt and **black pepper**

Hollandaise sauce
1 large **egg yolk**
1 teaspoon **lemon juice**
1 teaspoon **white wine**
   vinegar
¼ cup **butter**

Make the hollandaise sauce. Put the egg yolk into the small bowl of a food processor or a blender and season well with salt and pepper. Heat the lemon juice and vinegar in a small pan until just boiling. Switch on the processor and gradually add the vinegar mixture in a steady stream. Melt the butter in the pan and, with the processor switched on again, add this in a steady stream to give a smooth sauce.

Bring a large skillet of water to a boil, then turn down the heat to a bare simmer. Break the eggs into the water and allow to cook very gently for 2 minutes. Remove from the pan with a slotted spoon.

Butter the muffins and top with the ham, a poached egg, and a generous dollop of the sauce.

For salmon eggs benedict with tarragon hollandaise, replace the white wine vinegar with 1 teaspoon tarragon vinegar and stir 1 tablespoon chopped tarragon through the sauce. Cook the eggs in the same way, but use 2 oz smoked salmon instead of the prosciutto.

brie & semidried tomato omelet

Serves **2**
Preparation time **5 minutes**
Cooking time **5 minutes**

4 large **eggs**, beaten
1 tablespoon **butter**
2 oz **Brie**, sliced
1 oz **semidried tomatoes**
1 **scallion**, sliced
salt and **black pepper**

Put the eggs in a bowl and beat them. Season to taste with salt and pepper.

Heat the butter in a large skillet and add the egg mixture. Cook over a medium heat, gently pushing the mixture toward the center of the pan and tipping the runny mixture to fill the spaces. When it is almost set remove from the heat and layer over the remaining ingredients. Fold over and serve immediately.

For smoked haddock, chive, & sour cream omelet, mix together in a small bowl 4 oz poached and flaked smoked haddock, 1 tablespoon chopped chives, and 1 tablespoon sour cream. Season with plenty of black pepper. Make the omelet as above and replace the filling with the smoked haddock mixture. Fold over and serve immediately.

ricotta & pear drizzle

Serves **2**
Preparation time **3 minutes**
Cooking time **1–2 minutes**

½ cup **ricotta cheese**
4 thick slices of **all-butter brioche**
1 small, sweet **dessert pear**, cored and finely sliced
3 tablespoons **honey**, plus extra for drizzling

Spread the ricotta thickly over 2 slices of brioche and fan out the pear slices over the top. Drizzle with the honey and top with the remaining slices of brioche.

Toast in a sandwich grill for 1–2 minutes or according to the manufacturer's instructions until the bread is crisp and golden. Cut in half diagonally and serve immediately, drizzled with extra honey.

For fig & mascarpone drizzle, beat together 2 tablespoons mascarpone cheese, 2 teaspoons honey, and a pinch of ground cinnamon. Lightly toast one side of 4 thick slices of all-butter brioche. Spread the mascarpone mixture over the untoasted sides. Thinly slice a fresh fig and arrange the slices over the mascarpone, sprinkle with 1 teaspoon Demerara sugar and cook under a preheated hot broiler for about 1 minute. Serve immediately.

omelet arnold bennett

Serves **2**
Preparation time **15 minutes**
Cooking time **10 minutes**

5 oz **smoked haddock**
1 ¼ cups **fish stock**
2 tablespoons grated
   Parmesan cheese
6 **eggs**
2 tablespoons **cold water**
2 tablespoons **butter**
2 tablespoons **heavy cream**
salt and **black pepper**

Gently poach the haddock in the fish stock for 7–8 minutes or until just tender. Allow to cool then remove any skin and bones.

Flake the haddock, mix with the cheese, and season to taste with salt and pepper. Put the eggs into a bowl and lightly beat with the water.

Melt the butter in an omelet pan and pour in the egg mixture. When the eggs begin to set, put the fish and cheese on top. While they are still liquid, pour over the cream then put the pan under a preheated hot broiler for a few minutes until the top is golden brown. Do not fold the omelet but slide it on to a hot plate and serve immediately.

For bacon & leek omelet, make the omelet as above. In a skillet melt 1 tablespoon butter and fry 1 finely sliced leek. Broil 4 slices of bacon and chop. Sprinkle the cooked leek over the omelet with the chopped bacon and ¼ cup grated Gruyère cheese. Fold over the omelet and serve.

pancakes with fruit

Serves **2**
Preparation time **5 minutes**
Cooking time **5 minutes**

½ cup **all-purpose flour**
½ teaspoon **baking powder**
1 tablespoon **superfine sugar**
¼ cup **dried fruit**, such as
  cranberries
1 **egg**, beaten
3 tablespoons **milk**
1 tablespoon **unsalted butter**

Sift together the flour and baking powder and stir in the sugar and dried fruit. Add the egg and milk and beat to give a smooth batter.

Melt the butter in a skillet. Add spoonfuls of the mixture to the pan and cook for about 1 minute or until lightly browned (you should have sufficient batter for 6 pancakes). Once the surface is covered in bubbles, turn over and cook until lightly browned.

Serve immediately with honey, if desired.

For Stilton cheese pancakes, replace the sugar and cranberries with 1½ oz crumbled Stilton cheese and 2 finely sliced scallions, which should be added to the bowl with the flour and baking powder. Prepare and cook the batter as above, making about 6 pancakes in all. Serve with butter.

cranberry granola

Serves **2**
Preparation time **10 minutes**
Cooking time **4–6 hours**

¾ cup **rolled oats**
¼ cup **dried cranberries**
½ tablespoon **sunflower oil**
1 tablespoon **honey**
skim milk or **low-fat plain yogurt**, to serve

Put all the ingredients in a warm mixing bowl and stir until the oats are covered evenly with the oil and honey.

Turn out onto a nonstick baking sheet, making sure that there are no lumps. Put in the bottom of a warm oven, 225°F, for 4-6 hours, stirring occasionally to prevent sticking or browning.

When crispy, remove and allow to cool. Serve with skim milk or low-fat yogurt. Store in an airtight container. The mixture will keep fresh for several days if kept free of moisture.

For apricot & seed granola, mix 2 tablespoons chopped dried apricots, with the oats, sunflower oil, and honey. Add 1 tablespoon each pumpkin seeds, sunflower seeds, and sesame seeds. Cook and serve as above.

banana oat & almond muffins

Makes **12**
Preparation time **10 minutes**
Cooking time **20 minutes**

⅓ cup **butter**, melted
2 tablespoons **honey**
1 **egg**, beaten
⅔ cup **whole milk**
1 large **banana**, roughly
   chopped
1½ cups **self-rising flour**
¾ cup **rolled oats**
1 teaspoon **baking powder**
¼ cup **ground almonds**
¼ cup **slivered almonds**

Mix together the butter, honey, egg, and milk in a pitcher. Put the banana, flour, oats, baking powder, and ground and slivered almonds in a large bowl. Pour in the milk mixture and quickly mix together all the ingredients to give a fairly lumpy mixture (this will give the muffins their lightness).

Line a 12-hole muffin pan with paper cups and spoon in the batter. Bake in a preheated oven, 400°F, for about 20 minutes until golden. Serve with butter and honey. Leftover muffins can be frozen or stored in an airtight container for three days.

For pear, apricot, & almond muffins, replace the banana with a peeled and chopped pear, 2 fresh chopped apricots (or 4 ready-to-eat dried apricots), and add a few drops of almond extract to the mixture. Combine the fruit with the flour, oats, baking powder, and almonds and quickly mix in the butter, honey, egg, and milk as above. Cook as above.

stuffed mushrooms on toast

Serves **2**
Preparation time **5 minutes**
Cooking time **10–12 minutes**

1 tablespoon **olive oil**
4 large, **open-cap mushrooms**
2 oz **bacon**, chopped
2 oz **chorizo**, sliced
1 tablespoon **butter**
1 **garlic clove**, crushed (optional)
1 tablespoon chopped **parsley**

Heat the oil in a large skillet. Lightly fry the mushrooms in the oil for 2–3 minutes, turning once.

Put the mushrooms, gill side up, in an ovenproof dish (there is no need to remove the stalks). Fry the bacon and chorizo in the butter and garlic (if using) until the bacon has browned. Stir in the parsley.

Spoon the bacon mixture into the mushrooms and bake in a preheated oven, 400°F, for 10–12 minutes or until the mushrooms are cooked through. Serve with thick slices of multigrain or whole-wheat toast.

For spinach-stuffed mushrooms, omit the bacon and chorizo. Heat the butter and fry ½ small onion and the garlic for 2–3 minutes. Add 3 large handfuls of baby leaf spinach and a good grating of nutmeg and cook briefly until the spinach has just wilted. Put the mixture in the mushrooms and top with a grating of fresh Parmesan cheese. Cook as above.

berry breakfast

Serves **2**

Preparation time **15 minutes**, plus chilling

²/₃ cup **Greek** or **whole milk yogurt**

1 tablespoon **honey**

1 ½ cups **raspberries**

3 tablespoons **rolled oats**

Put the yogurt in a large bowl and fold in the honey.

Divide one-third of the raspberries between 2 serving glasses. Cover with half the yogurt mixture. Sprinkle with some of the oats and more raspberries, dividing them evenly between the glasses.

Repeat the layers, finishing with oats and a few raspberries. Chill in the refrigerator for 30 minutes before serving.

For mango breakfast, puree the flesh of 1 large, ripe mango. Add the mango instead of the raspberries to the yogurt, honey, and oats as above.

kedgeree

Serves **2**
Preparation time **10 minutes**
Cooking time **15 minutes**

7 oz **smoked haddock**
¾ cup **milk**
1 **bay leaf**
2 teaspoons **vegetable oil**
1 small **onion**, chopped
½ cup **basmati rice**
½ teaspoon **curry powder**
2 **hard-cooked eggs**, roughly
  chopped
1 tablespoon chopped
  parsley

Put the haddock in a small saucepan with the milk and bay leaf, simmer for 3 minutes or until just cooked, and remove the fish from the milk, reserving the milk. Flake the fish and set aside.

Heat the oil in a medium skillet. Add the onion and fry for 3 minutes. Add the rice and curry powder and fry for a minute more.

Make the reserved milk up to 1 cup with water and pour it over the rice. Cover and cook for 12 minutes until the rice is cooked and fluffy. Add the remaining ingredients and the flaked haddock, stir to combine, and serve.

For mackerel & pea kedgeree, flake 7 oz peppered smoked mackerel instead of the haddock and use 1 cup water to cook the rice. Add ⅔ cup frozen peas to the rice 3 minutes before the end of cooking time.

gravlax & cream cheese bagels

Serves **2**
Preparation time **14 minutes**
Cooking time **14–16 minutes**

2 **poppy and sesame seed bagels**, cut in half horizontally
½ cup **cream cheese**
6 oz **gravlax**, finely sliced
2 tablespoons chopped **chives**
black pepper, plus extra to serve

Put the bagels, cut side down, on a sandwich grill. Without closing the lid, allow them to toast for 2–3 minutes until golden. Remove from the grill.

Spread the bases with the cream cheese and then top with the gravlax. Sprinkle the chopped chives over the bagel and season with black pepper.

Top with the bagel lids and return to the sandwich grill. Lower the top plate and toast for 2–3 minutes or according to the manufacturer's instructions until golden and crispy. Serve immediately with a sprinkling of black pepper.

For salt beef & pickle bagels, cut 2 bagels in half horizontally and toast them on both sides. Layer 2 of the bagel halves with 2 oz sliced salt beef and 2 sliced pickled gherkins. Mix together 1 tablespoon light sour cream and 1 teaspoon Dijon mustard and spoon the mixture over the beef and gherkins. Garnish with watercress and top with the other bagel halves.

big raspberry muffins

Makes **6**
Preparation time **5 minutes**
Cooking time **15–20 minutes**

1 ¾ cups **all-purpose flour**
⅓ cup **superfine sugar**
2 tablespoons **ground almonds**
2 teaspoons **baking powder**
grated zest of 1 **lemon**
⅔ cup **buttermilk**
1 **egg**, beaten
¼ cup **butter**, melted
1 ¼ cups fresh or frozen **raspberries**

Mix together the flour, sugar, ground almonds, baking powder, and lemon zest in a large bowl. In a separate bowl mix together the remaining ingredients, then fold into the flour mixture to give a slightly lumpy texture.

Spoon the batter into 6 large muffin paper bake cups set in a muffin pan and cook in a preheated oven, 350°F, for 15–20 minutes until golden and risen. These muffins can be frozen or stored in an airtight tin.

For black currant crunch muffins, make the batter as above, replacing the raspberries with 1 ⅔ cups fresh black currants. Spoon the batter into 6 muffin paper bake cups and sprinkle the top of the uncooked muffins with 1 tablespoon chopped hazelnuts and 1 tablespoon Demerara sugar. Cook as above.

fruit & nut bars

Makes **8**
Preparation time **10 minutes**
Cooking time **15 minutes**

½ cup **butter**, plus extra for greasing
4 tablespoons **maple syrup**
2 tablespoons **light brown sugar**
1½ cups **rolled oats**
½ cup **steel-cut oats**
⅓ cup chopped **mixed nuts**
1 cup **mixed dried fruit**, such as figs, dates, ready-to-eat apricots, and cranberries, chopped
2 tablespoons **sunflower seeds**

Lightly grease an 8 inch square, nonstick baking pan and line the base with nonstick parchment paper. In a saucepan melt the butter, syrup, and sugar together. Stir in all the remaining ingredients except the sunflower seeds, then press the mixture into the prepared pan.

Sprinkle with the sunflower seeds, then bake in a preheated oven, 400°F, for 15 minutes or until golden. Cut into 8 bars, allow to cool, then serve. These bars can be stored in an airtight container for up to one week.

For speedy bar cookies, melt ¾ cup unsalted butter with ¾ cup dark brown sugar in a saucepan. Remove from the heat and stir through 2½ cups square rolled oats. Press the mixture into a lined and greased 8 in baking pan and cook in a preheated oven, 350°F, for 15 minutes. Cut into 12 bars and allow to cool.

hot vanilla

Serves **2**
Preparation time **5 minutes**,
    plus standing
Cooking time **2 minutes**

1 ¼ cups **milk**
½ cup chopped **white
    chocolate**
½ teaspoon **vanilla extract**
unsweetened **cocoa powder**,
    for sprinkling
vanilla bean, to decorate
    (optional)

Pour the milk into a saucepan and bring it almost
to a boil. Remove the pan from the heat and tip in
the chocolate. Let stand for 2–3 minutes, stirring
frequently, until the chocolate has melted.

Add the vanilla extract to the saucepan. Beat with a
balloon whisk or an immersion blender until the milk is
smooth and topped with a thick foam.

Pour the hot milk between 2 mugs and serve
sprinkled with cocoa powder. Decorate with a vanilla
bean, if desired.

For hot mint chocolate, heat 1 ¼ cups milk and
add ½ cup chopped semisweet chocolate. Let
stand, stirring, until the chocolate has melted, add
peppermint essence to taste (about ½ teaspoon),
and beat as above.

light bites

vietnamese crab lettuce rolls

Serves **2**
Preparation time **10 minutes**

2 x 5½ oz cans **crabmeat**,
  drained, or the equivalent
  weight **fresh crab**
1 **red chili**, seeded and finely
  chopped
handful of **cilantro**, chopped
1 tablespoon chopped **mint**
grated zest and juice of **1 lime**
½ inch **fresh ginger root**,
  finely grated
4 **iceberg lettuce leaves**,
  halved

Chili dipping sauce
1 teaspoon **brown sugar**
1 tablespoon **rice vinegar**
juice of ½ **lime**
1 teaspoon **soy sauce**
1 **red chili**, finely chopped
1 **scallion**, finely sliced

Mix together the crab, chili, cilantro, mint, lime zest and juice, and the ginger in a bowl.

Spoon equal amounts of the mixture onto the lettuce leaves. Roll them up and set them aside.

Make the dipping sauce. In a small bowl mix together the sugar, vinegar, lime juice, and soy sauce until the sugar has dissolved. Stir in the chili and scallion.

Serve the crab lettuce rolls with the chili sauce for dipping in a separate dish.

For crab & noodle lettuce rolls, cook 4 oz rice noodles in boiling water according to the instructions on the package. Allow the noodles to cool, then combine them with the crab, cilantro, mint, lemon zest and juice, and ginger as above. Wrap this mixture in halved iceberg lettuce leaves and serve with the chili dipping sauce.

asparagus and fontina toastie

Serves **2**
Preparation time **5 minutes**
Cooking time **3–4 minutes**

4 oz trimmed **asparagus spears**
4 thin slices of **Black Forest ham**
3 oz **fontina cheese**, grated
small handful of **arugula**
2 **vine-ripened tomatoes**, sliced
4 slices of **sourdough bread**
2 tablespoons **olive oil**
2 teaspoons **balsamic vinegar**

Steam the asparagus in a steamer for 3–4 minutes so that it is still quite firm. Allow to cool.

Arrange the ham, grated fontina, arugula, asparagus, and tomatoes over 2 slices of sourdough bread. Drizzle with the oil and balsamic vinegar and top with the remaining slices of bread.

Toast the sandwiches in a sandwich grill for about 3–4 minutes or according to the manufacturer's instructions until the bread is golden and the cheese has melted. Serve immediately.

For salmon & cream cheese toastie, spread 2 tablespoons cream cheese over 2 slices of sourdough bread. Arrange 1½ oz smoked salmon over the cheese, squeeze over a little lemon juice, and season well with black pepper. Top each with another slice of sourdough bread and cook in a sandwich grill as above.

trout pâté & sesame crackers

Serves **2**

Preparation time **15 minutes**, plus chilling

Cooking time **10 minutes**

Crackers

1 cup **all-purpose flour**

¼ cup **butter**

2 tablespoons grated **Parmesan cheese**

1 **egg yolk**, beaten

1 tablespoon **sesame seeds**

Pâté

7 oz **hot-smoked trout fillets**

1 tablespoon **capers**, drained

2 tablespoons **sour cream**

1 teaspoon **horseradish sauce**

1 teaspoon chopped **dill weed**

Put the flour and butter in a bowl and blend together with your fingertips until the mixture resembles bread crumbs. Stir in the Parmesan and enough egg yolk to bring the mixture together into a dough.

Roll out the pastry on a lightly floured surface, brush with the remaining egg, and sprinkle with the sesame seeds. Cut the dough into about 20 rounds with a cookie cutter, transfer to nonstick baking sheets, and bake in a preheated oven, 400°F, for about 10 minutes. Allow to cool on a cooling rack.

Put the trout, capers, sour cream, horseradish, and dill in a food processor or blender and process for about 10 seconds until the ingredients are combined but still retain some texture. Chill for about 30 minutes, then serve with the crackers. Uneaten crackers can be stored in an airtight container for a few days.

For roasted pepper pâté, put a large red bell pepper under a hot broiler and cook until blackened. Transfer to a bowl and cover with plastic wrap. Allow to cool, then remove the skin and finely chop the flesh. Beat the pepper flesh into 6 tablespoons cream cheese and 1 tablespoon green pesto. Transfer the pâté to a bowl, chill for 30 minutes, and serve with sesame crackers.

bean soup with guacamole

Serves **2**
Preparation time **10 minutes**
Cooking time **15 minutes**

1 teaspoon **olive oil**
1 **onion**, chopped
1 **garlic clove**, crushed
1 **red chili**, seeded and
  chopped
13 oz can **mixed beans**,
  rinsed and drained
7½ oz can **chopped
  tomatoes**
1¼ cups **vegetable stock**
  (see pages 94–5 for
  homemade)
salt and **black pepper**

Guacamole
1 **avocado**, skinned and pitted
2 **scallions**, finely sliced
2 **tomatoes**, chopped
1 tablespoon chopped
  cilantro
juice of ½ **lime**

Make the guacamole. Roughly chop the avocado flesh and mash it together with the scallions, tomatoes, cilantro, and lime juice. Set aside.

Heat the oil in a medium saucepan. Add the onion, garlic, and chili and fry for 2–3 minutes or until softened. Add the beans, tomatoes, and stock, bring to a boil, and simmer for 10 minutes.

Transfer three-quarters of the soup to a food processor or blender and process until almost smooth. Add to the reserved soup and stir to combine. Season to taste with salt and pepper and warm through.

Serve the soup with the guacamole and tortilla chips.

For smoked bacon & bean soup with guacamole, add 2 oz chopped bacon to the saucepan with the onion, garlic, and chili, and cook for 2–3 minutes. Continue as above. Garnish with a spoonful of sour cream and serve with the guacamole.

crunchy thai-style salad

Serves **2**
Preparation time **10 minutes**

2 **carrots**
1 **zucchini**
½ small **red cabbage**, finely
  shredded
1 **yellow bell pepper**, cored,
  seeded, and thinly sliced
4 **scallions**, finely sliced
2 tablespoons chopped
  cilantro
5 oz **rice noodles**

Dressing
1 **red chili**, seeded and
  chopped
4 tablespoons **fish sauce**
  (nam pla)
grated zest and juice of 1 **lime**
2 tablespoons **superfine**
  sugar

Use a potato peeler to shred the carrots and zucchini into fine slices. Toss together the sliced vegetables with the cabbage, pepper, scallions, and cilantro.

Cook the noodles in boiling water according to the instructions on the package, drain, and allow to cool.

Make the dressing by beating together the chili, fish sauce, lime zest and juice, and sugar in a small bowl.

Mix the noodles with the vegetables. Toss the dressing through the salad and serve.

For crunchy coleslaw salad, toss together the sliced carrots, zucchini, cabbage, pepper, and scallions as above. In a separate bowl beat together 1 tablespoon yogurt, 1 tablespoon mayonnaise, 1 teaspoon mustard, and a good squeeze of lemon juice. Stir this dressing into the vegetables, sprinkle with 2 tablespoons coriander seeds and serve.

lamb tortilla wraps

Serves **2**
Preparation time **5 minutes**
Cooking time **8–10 minutes**

1 teaspoon **olive oil**
1 **garlic clove**, finely chopped
1 small **onion**, finely chopped
4 oz lean **lamb leg steaks**,
  cut into small strips
2 oz **mushrooms**, finely
  chopped
½ small **red bell pepper**,
  cored, seeded, and sliced
1 tablespoon chopped
  parsley
1 tablespoon chopped **mint**
¼ cup **basmati rice**, cooked
2 tablespoons **lemon juice**
2 tablespoons **Greek** or
  whole milk yogurt
1 tablespoon **mint sauce**
4 flour **tortillas** or **flatbreads**
2 inches **cucumber**, cut into
  strips

Make the filling. Heat the oil in a nonstick wok or skillet and cook the garlic, onion, and lamb strips for 3–4 minutes until brown. Add the mushrooms and pepper and cook for 2–3 minutes. Stir in the herbs, rice, and lemon juice. Heat for an additional 1–2 minutes.

Mix together the yogurt and mint sauce in a bowl.

Assemble the wraps. Lay the flour tortillas on a clean work surface. Spread a dessertspoon of the yogurt mixture over each tortilla, top with a large spoonful of the filling and a few strips of cucumber.

Fold up to make neat rolls and serve immediately with an arugula salad.

For chicken tortilla wraps, use either 8 oz chicken strips or the same weight of boneless, skinless chicken breasts, cut into strips. Cook the garlic and onions as above. Add the chicken to the pan and stir-fry until cooked through. Add the vegetables and remaining ingredients to the pan. Make the tortillas as above and serve with mayonnaise or salsa verde (see page 100–1 for homemade).

shrimp & watercress mayo

Serves **2**
Preparation time **15 minutes**

3 tablespoons **mayonnaise**
large handful of **watercress**,
    plus extra to serve
2 **gherkins**, roughly chopped
grated zest and juice of
    ½ **lemon**
8 oz **jumbo shrimp**, cooked
salt and **black pepper**

Put the mayonnaise, watercress, gherkins, and lemon zest and juice into a food processor or blender and process until almost smooth. Season to taste with salt and pepper.

Toss the jumbo shrimp in the dressing to coat and serve with fresh, crusty bread and extra watercress.

For chicken & pesto mayo, stir 1 tablespoon pesto through 2 tablespoons mayonnaise. Toss 2 cooked and chopped chicken breasts through the dressing and serve with pita bread.

walnut & pear salad

Serves **2**
Preparation time **10 minutes**

1 tablespoon **olive oil**
7 oz **ciabatta**, torn into bite-size pieces
1 **romaine lettuce**, torn into bite-size pieces
1 large, ripe **pear**, cored and finely sliced
¼ cup toasted **walnuts**, roughly chopped

Dressing
3 tablespoons **sour cream**
2 oz **Stilton cheese**, crumbled
1 **anchovy**, drained and chopped
2 tablespoons **water**
black pepper

Drizzle the oil over the ciabatta pieces, then toast the bread under a preheated hot broiler until golden all over. Toss the croutons together with the lettuce, pear, and walnuts.

Make the dressing. Mix together the sour cream, Stilton, anchovy, and water in a small bowl and season with plenty of pepper.

Spoon the dressing over the salad and serve.

For chicken & pancetta salad, prepare all the salad ingredients as above but omit the pear. Heat 1 teaspoon olive oil in a skillet. Add 1 thinly sliced chicken breast and fry for 3–4 minutes. Set aside. Add 4 slices of pancetta to the pan and cook for about 1 minute until crisp. Mix the chicken with the salad and serve with the pancetta on top.

toasted peanut & wild rice salad

Serves **2**
Preparation time **5 minutes**
Cooking time **30 minutes**

½ cup **basmati rice**
2 tablespoons **wild rice**
1 bunch of **scallions**, chopped
⅔ cup **golden raisins**
½ cup toasted **peanuts**
4 tablespoons **balsamic vinegar**
1 tablespoon **sunflower oil**

Cook both types of rice according to the instructions on the packages. Rinse in cold water and drain thoroughly.

Mix together the cooked rice, scallions, golden raisins, and peanuts in a large bowl.

Pour the vinegar and oil into a small bowl and beat together, then stir the dressing into the rice mixture. Serve with a salad of crisp green leaves.

For trout & wild rice salad, cook the rice as above and add the scallions, golden raisins, and peanuts. Flake 5 oz smoked trout fillet and stir through the rice salad with 1 ¼ cups chopped watercress. Dress and serve as above.

eggplant pâté

Serves **2**
Preparation time **10 minutes**
Cooking time **30–40 minutes**

2 **eggplants**, cubed
2 **garlic cloves**, sliced
2 tablespoons **olive oil**
1 teaspoon **cumin seeds**
pinch of **dried red pepper flakes**
1 tablespoon chopped **cilantro**
salt and **black pepper**

Put the eggplant in a baking pan and add the garlic. Drizzle over the oil and then sprinkle with the cumin seeds and pepper flakes. Season well with salt and pepper.

Cook in a preheated oven, 400°F, for 35–40 minutes until tender and golden.

Transfer the mixture to a food processor or blender and process for a few seconds so that the mixture still has some texture. Allow to cool, then stir through the chopped cilantro. Serve with toasted pita bread.

For Mediterranean pâté, cook 1 eggplant and 1 chopped yellow bell pepper with garlic as above, sprinkling the leaves from a sprig of lemon thyme over the olive oil instead of the cumin and pepper flakes. Allow to cool then transfer to a food processor or blender and process with 3 tablespoons cream cheese to make a smooth mixture.

cheesy tortillas with tuna salsa

Serves **2**
Preparation time **10 minutes**
Cooking time **5 minutes**

10 oz fresh **tuna**, cut into
small cubes
1 **avocado**, peeled, pitted, and
chopped
1 large **tomato**, chopped
½ **green chili**, seeded and
chopped
large handful of **watercress**,
chopped
salt and **black pepper**

Tortillas
2 large **flour tortillas**
2 oz **mozzarella cheese**,
finely sliced
2 **scallions**, sliced
1 tablespoon chopped
cilantro

Mix together the tuna, avocado, tomato, chili, and watercress in a nonmetallic dish and set aside for 10 minutes.

Meanwhile, heat a large skillet. Place one tortilla on a cutting board. Layer the mozzarella, scallions, and cilantro on top of the tortilla. Put the other tortilla on top, press down a little, and transfer to the skillet. Cook for 1 minute, then turn over and cook for a minute more. Cut into wedges and serve with the tuna salsa.

For cheesy tortillas with goats cheese & red pepper salsa, roughly chop 5 oz goats cheese. Halve, core, and seed 1 red bell pepper and roughly chop the flesh. Toss the cheese and pepper together with 1 chopped avocado, 1 chopped large tomato, ½ green chili, seeded and chopped, and a large handful of watercress. Serve with cheesy tortillas prepared as above.

chicken & sweet potato soup

Serves **2**
Preparation time **10 minutes**
Cooking time **15 minutes**

2 teaspoons **olive oil**
1 small **onion**, chopped
1 **garlic clove**, crushed
1 **red chili**, seeded and
  chopped
1 large **sweet potato**, peeled
  and cubed
1 large boneless, skinless
  chicken breast, chopped
1¾ cups **coconut milk**
2½ cups **chicken stock** (see
  pages 13 and 146)
1 tablespoon chopped
  cilantro
salt

Heat the oil in a nonstick skillet. Add the onion, garlic, and chili and fry for 3 minutes until softened. Add the sweet potato and chicken and continue to fry for 2–3 minutes until the chicken is browned all over.

Add the coconut milk and stock to the pan, bring to a boil, cover, and simmer for 15 minutes until the potato is tender.

Transfer to a food processor or blender and process until smooth. Season to taste with salt, stir through the chopped cilantro, and serve.

For spiced butternut squash soup, cook the onion, garlic and chili as above, but omit the chicken and replace the sweet potato with 1 medium peeled and chopped butternut squash. Add the coconut milk and 1¼ cups vegetable stock (see pages 94–5 for homemade) instead of the chicken stock. Bring to a boil and finish as above.

herbed citrus chicken salad

Serves **2**
Preparation time **20 minutes**,
  plus marinating
Cooking time **10–15 minutes**

2 boneless, skinless **chicken breasts**
4 cups shredded **romaine lettuce**
4 cups shredded **radicchio**
½ large **avocado**, pitted, peeled, and thinly sliced
1 tablespoon chopped **cilantro**

Lemon cumin dressing
2 tablespoons **lemon juice**
½ teaspoon **soy sauce**
1 teaspoon **ground cumin**
6 tablespoons **olive oil**

Orange & coriander marinade
2 tablespoons **olive oil**
½ tablespoon **lemon juice**
½ tablespoon **orange juice**
2 **garlic cloves**, chopped
½ teaspoon **ground coriander**
½ teaspoon **ground cumin**
¼ teaspoon **cinnamon**

Make the marinade. Mix together all the ingredients in a small bowl. Put the chicken breasts in a nonmetallic dish and, reserving 2 tablespoons for basting, pour the rest of the marinade over the chicken, coating it thoroughly. Cover and refrigerate for 20 minutes.

Meanwhile, make the dressing. Mix together the lemon juice, soy sauce, cumin, and oil in a bowl. Set aside.

Remove the chicken from the marinade, reserving the marinade, and place it on a foil-lined baking sheet. Put the baking sheet on a rack and place it about 6 inches below a preheated broiler. Cook the chicken, turning occasionally and brushing it with the reserved marinade, for about 10 minutes or until a skewer will easily go into the chicken and the juices run clear.

Put the shredded romaine and radicchio lettuces in a large bowl. Toss with 1–2 tablespoons of the dressing then arrange on a large platter. Cut the chicken breasts into ½ inch slices and set them on the lettuce.

Garnish with the avocado slices. Pour the remaining dressing over, sprinkle with chopped cilantro, and serve.

For herbed citrus tofu salad, cut 7 oz tofu into thin slices. Make the marinade as above and marinate the tofu for at least 20 minutes. Cook the tofu under a preheated hot broiler for 2–3 minutes. Prepare the salad as above and dress with lemon cumin dressing. Toss the salad and dressing together to mix, add the tofu and serve, garnished with chopped fresh cilantro.

lentil & tomato salad with egg

Serves **2**
Preparation time **5 minutes**
Cooking time **5 minutes**

2 teaspoons **olive oil**
4 **scallions**, sliced
1 **garlic clove**, crushed
13 oz can **puy lentils** or
    green lentils, rinsed and
    drained
10 **cherry tomatoes**, halved
1 tablespoon chopped
    parsley
1 tablespoon **balsamic**
    vinegar
2 **eggs**

Heat the oil in a nonstick skillet. Add the scallions and garlic and fry for 1 minute. Add the lentils, tomatoes, parsley, and vinegar and warm through.

Meanwhile, bring a large pan of lightly salted water to a boil. Stir the water to make a gentle "whirlpool" and crack in an egg, allowing the white to wrap around the yolk. Cook for 3 minutes, remove from the pan, and cook the other egg in the same way.

Serve the eggs on a bed of lentils with some crusty bread to mop up the juices.

For chorizo & rice salad with egg, replace the lentils with 2¼ cups cooked basmati and wild rice (buy ready-mixed and cook according to the instructions on the package). Continue as above and serve topped with 8 slices of broiled chorizo and a poached egg on each serving.

stilton welsh rarebit

Serves **2**
Preparation time **5 minutes**
Cooking time **5 minutes**

1 tablespoon **butter**
4 **scallions**, sliced
4 oz **Stilton cheese**, crumbled
1 **egg yolk**
a little **milk**
2 slices of **multigrain bread**,
  lightly toasted
2 slices of **bacon**, broiled

Heat the butter in a small saucepan and fry the scallions for 2–3 minutes until softened. Allow to cool, then mix with the Stilton and egg yolk, adding enough milk to make a spreadable mixture.

Spread the mixture over the toast and cook under a preheated hot broiler for about 2 minutes until golden and bubbling. Serve topped with the broiled bacon.

For Cheddar rarebit, ¾ cup grated cheddar cheese instead of the Stilton and add ½ teaspoon English mustard to the mixture before spreading it over the toast. Broil under a preheated hot broiler and serve as above.

chili bean con carne

Serves **2**
Preparation time **30 minutes**
Cooking time **55 minutes**

1 tablespoon **olive oil**
1 small **onion**, finely chopped
1 **garlic clove**, crushed
8 oz **ground beef**
1 tablespoon **tomato paste**
1 large **red chili**, chopped
½ teaspoon **hot chili powder**
1 teaspoon dried **mixed herbs**
7 oz can **chopped tomatoes**
7½ oz can **baked beans**
black pepper

To serve
6 tablespoons **sour cream**
1 tablespoon chopped **flat-leaf parsley**
½ cup grated **cheddar cheese**
jalapeño peppers (optional)

Make the chili. Heat the oil in a large pan, add the onion and garlic, and cook over a medium heat for 5 minutes or until softened. Increase the heat to high and add the ground beef. Fry, stirring, for 5 minutes or until browned all over.

Stir in the tomato paste, chili, chili powder, and mixed herbs and continue to cook for 5 minutes. Add the tomatoes and baked beans, bring to a boil, cover, and simmer for 30 minutes.

Transfer the chili to a serving bowl and top with sour cream. Garnish with pepper and chopped parsley and serve with cheesy scones (see below) and separate bowls of grated cheese and jalapeño peppers, if liked.

For scones, to serve as an accompaniment, mix together 2 cups all-purpose flour and 2 teaspoons baking powder in a large bowl. Blend in ⅓ cup diced butter and add ½ cup sharp, grated cheddar cheese. Make a well in the center and pour in 1 beaten egg and 3 tablespoons milk. Use a knife to mix the dough until it comes together. Turn out the dough onto a lightly floured surface and roll it out to about ¼ inch thick. Cut out 8 rounds, each 2 inches in diameter, and place them on a baking sheet. Brush the tops with a little milk and bake in a preheated oven, 400°F, for 12 minutes or until they sound hollow when tapped.

spinach & feta tarts

Makes **4**
Preparation time **10 minutes**,
  plus chilling
Cooking time **25 minutes**

Pastry
1¾ cups **all-purpose flour**
½ cup cold **butter**, diced
about 6 tablespoons **cold
  water**

Filling
3 cups **baby leaf spinach**
⅔ cup **sour cream**
1 **egg**, beaten
2 oz **feta cheese**, crumbled
grated **nutmeg**
black pepper

Sift the flour into a large bowl, add the butter, and blend in with your fingertips until the mixture resembles fine bread crumbs. Add enough cold water to make a ball. Bring the dough together, wrap in plastic wrap, and chill for 30 minutes.

Divide the pastry into 4, roll out each piece and use it to line 4 lightly greased tartlet pans, each 3½ inches across. Bake blind (i.e. bake the empty cases without filling) in a preheated oven, 400°F, for 5 minutes. Then remove the tart shells, but leave the oven on.

Meanwhile, put the spinach in a large colander, pour over boiling water to wilt the leaves, then squeeze out any liquid. Divide the spinach among the tart shells. Beat together the sour cream and egg and season well with grated nutmeg and black pepper. Stir through the feta. Pour the mixture into the tart shells (still in their pans) and cook for 15–20 minutes or until golden and puffy. Serve with a side salad.

For trout & asparagus tarts, make the tart shells as above. Halve 8 trimmed asparagus spears and simmer in boiling water for 1 minute, then drain. Arrange the asparagus in the tart shells with 3 oz flaked smoked trout. Mix together ⅔ cup sour cream and 1 egg as above and pour the mixture over the asparagus. Cook as above and serve warm.

stilton & pancetta bruschetta

Serves **2**
Preparation time **5 minutes**
Cooking time **5 minutes**

1 tablespoon **olive oil**
1 **garlic clove**, crushed
4 oz **pancetta**, cut into small
  cubes
8 oz mixed **mushrooms**,
  sliced
4 tablespoons **heavy cream**
1 oz **Stilton cheese**, crumbled
1 tablespoon chopped
  parsley
4 slices of **ciabatta**, toasted

Heat the oil in a skillet. Add the garlic and pancetta and fry for 1–2 minutes. Stir in the mushrooms and fry for an additional 2–3 minutes until cooked.

Stir in the cream and crumbled Stilton and cook for 1 minute to warm through. Add the parsley to the mixture, stir to combine, and serve on 2 slices of toasted ciabatta for each person.

For Stilton & pancetta pasta, cook 10 oz pasta in boiling water according to the instructions on the package. Meanwhile, cook 1 crushed garlic clove, 3 oz pancetta, and 8 oz mushrooms as above. Stir the cream and Stilton through the mushrooms and warm. Drain the pasta and mix with the cream and mushroom mixture. Garnish with chopped parsley and serve with a green salad.

summer vegetable soup

Serves **2**
Preparation time **10 minutes**
Cooking time **15 minutes**

1 teaspoon **olive oil**
½ **leek,** finely sliced
½ large **potato,** chopped
7 oz **mixed summer vegetables,** such as peas, asparagus, fava beans, and zucchini
1 tablespoon chopped **mint**
1¾ cups **vegetable stock** (see right for homemade)
1 tablespoon **sour cream**
salt (optional) and **black pepper**

Heat the oil in a medium saucepan, add the leek and potato, and fry for 2–3 minutes until softened.

Add the vegetables to the pan with the mint and the stock and bring to a boil. Reduce the heat and simmer for 10 minutes.

Transfer the soup to a food processor or blender and process until smooth. Return to the pan with the sour cream and season with salt (if desired) and pepper. Heat through and serve.

For homemade vegetable stock, heat 1 tablespoon olive oil in a large saucepan. Add 1 chopped onion, 1 chopped carrot, 4 chopped celery sticks, and any available vegetable trimmings (such as celery leaves, onion skins, and tomato skins) and fry for 2–3 minutes. Add 1 bouquet garni and season well with salt and pepper. Add 7 cups water and bring to a boil. Reduce the heat and simmer gently for 1½ hours. Strain. This makes about 5 cups of stock.

roasted peppers with haloumi

Serves **2**
Preparation time **10 minutes**
Cooking time **25 minutes**

8 **anchovy fillets**, halved
1 **garlic clove**, sliced
8 oz **cherry tomatoes**, halved
1 tablespoon **pesto** (see
  pages 12–13 for
  homemade)
1 **red bell pepper**, halved,
  cored, and seeded
1 **yellow bell pepper**, halved,
  cored, and seeded
4 oz **haloumi cheese**, cut into
  4 slices
1 tablespoon **olive oil**
1 handful **arugula**
1 tablespoon toasted **pine
  nuts**

Mix together the anchovies, garlic, tomatoes, and pesto.

Put the peppers on a baking sheet, cut sides up, and fill with the anchovy mixture. Lay a slice of haloumi over each and drizzle over the oil.

Cook in a preheated oven, 425°F, for 20–25 minutes until the peppers are tender and the cheese is golden.

Top with the arugula, sprinkle with the pine nuts, and serve.

For chicken, pepper, & haloumi pasta, halve, core, and seed 1 red and 1 yellow bell pepper. Place the pepper halves on a baking sheet and broil until the skin is blackened. Put them in a bowl, cover with plastic wrap, and allow to cool. Remove the skin from the peppers and tear the flesh into strips. Cook 8 oz pasta shapes in boiling water according to the instructions on the package. Drain. Mix together the peppers, anchovies, garlic, tomatoes, and pesto and mix through the pasta. Sprinkle with 4 oz torn haloumi and serve with arugula and toasted pine nuts.

spinach & lima bean frittata

Serves **2**

Preparation time **10 minutes**

Cooking time **10 minutes**

1 teaspoon **olive oil**

1 **onion**, sliced

13 oz can **lima beans**, rinsed and drained

4 cups **baby spinach leaves**

4 **eggs**, beaten

3 tablespoons **ricotta cheese**

salt (optional) and **black pepper**

Heat the oil in a medium skillet. Add the onion and fry for 3–4 minutes until softened. Add the beans and spinach and heat gently for 2–3 minutes until the spinach has wilted.

Pour over the eggs, then spoon over the ricotta and season with salt (if desired) and pepper. Cook until almost set, then place under a preheated hot broiler and cook for 1–2 minutes until golden and set. Serve with a tomato and red onion salad.

For Stilton & broccoli frittata, heat 1 teaspoon olive oil in a skillet and fry 1 sliced onion until softened. Add ½ cup small, cooked broccoli florets and fry for 2 more minutes. Add the beaten eggs and sprinkle through 3 oz crumbled Stilton cheese. Cook as above until almost set then transfer to a hot broiler and cook until golden.

crispy chicken with salsa verde

Serves **2**
Preparation time **10 minutes**,
  plus marinating
Cooking time **10 minutes**

2 boneless **chicken breasts**,
  skin on
1 teaspoon **olive oil**
1 **garlic clove**, crushed
1 tablespoon **soy sauce**

Salsa verde
1 handful **fresh mixed herbs**
  (such as parsley, thyme, and
  basil)
1 **garlic clove**, roughly
  chopped
2 **cornichons**
1 tablespoon drained **capers**
1 **anchovy**
2 tablespoons **olive oil**
1 teaspoon **white wine**
  vinegar

Make 3 slashes across the skin side of the chicken breasts and transfer to a nonmetallic dish.

Mix together the oil, garlic, and soy sauce, pour the mixture over the chicken and allow to marinate for 10 minutes.

Meanwhile, make the salsa verde. Mix all the ingredients together in a blender or food processor until they form a chunky paste. Chill until required.

Heat a griddle pan or heavy skillet, add the marinated chicken breasts, skin side down, and fry for 2–3 minutes. Turn and cook for an additional 3–4 minutes until they are cooked through.

Serve the chicken with a spoonful of salsa verde and some potatoes.

For Greek salad, to serve as an accompaniment, toss together 8 oz halved cherry tomatoes, ¼ chopped cucumber, 1 small sliced red onion, and 4 oz crumbled feta cheese. Drizzle over 1 tablespoon of olive oil and 1 teaspoon red wine vinegar and sprinkle with 1 tablespoon chopped fresh oregano. Season with salt and pepper to taste.

Italian bean & artichoke salad

Serves **2**
Preparation time **10 minutes**

13 oz can **artichoke hearts**
1 small **red onion**, sliced
3 oz ball **mozzarella cheese**,
  cubed
13 oz can **cannellini beans**,
  drained and rinsed
2 cups **arugula**

Dressing
1 **red chili**, finely chopped
1 teaspoon **cider vinegar**
1 teaspoon **Dijon mustard**
1 teaspoon **superfine sugar**
1 tablespoon **olive oil**
1 tablespoon chopped **fresh
  mixed herbs** (such as
  parsley, cilantro, and basil)

Make the dressing. Beat together the vinegar, mustard, sugar, oil, and chopped herbs in a small bowl. Set aside.

Drain the artichoke hearts and mix them with the onion, mozzarella, and beans. Add the arugula and combine.

Stir the dressing through the salad and serve.

For quick bean & feta salad, cut 2 thick slices of bread into cubes. Brush them with 1 tablespoon olive oil, transfer to a roasting pan, and cook in a preheated oven, 400°F, for 10–15 minutes until golden. Combine 7 oz can mixed bean salad with 2 oz chopped feta cheese. Serve with chopped romaine lettuce and a handful of croutons.

endive, mackerel, & orange salad

Serves **2**
Preparation time **10 minutes**

2 heads of **Belgian endive**
2 **mackerel** fillets, flaked
2 **oranges**, segmented
handful of **watercress**

Dressing
juice of **1 orange**
1 tablespoon **olive oil**
1 teaspoon **wholegrain mustard**
1 teaspoon **honey**

Separate the Belgian endive into individual leaves and mix them in a large bowl with the mackerel, orange segments, and watercress.

Make the dressing. Beat together the orange juice, oil, mustard, and honey.

Drizzle the dressing over the salad and serve with crusty bread.

For Gruyère & mixed seed salad, combine the leaves of 2 heads of Belgian endive with 3 oz chopped Gruyère cheese and about 1/4 cup toasted mixed seeds and the orange and watercress as above. Drizzle over the dressing and serve.

chèvre & asparagus panini

Serves **2**
Preparation time **5 minutes**
Cooking time **18–20 minutes**

5 oz trimmed **asparagus spears**
2 tablespoons **olive oil**
4 oz **soft mild goats cheese**
4 slices of French-style **walnut bread**
3 oz **firm goats cheese** with rind, sliced
1 teaspoon chopped **lemon thyme**
salt and **black pepper**

To serve
large handful of **arugula leaves**
2 teaspoons **truffle oil**

Toss the asparagus spears in the oil, season well, and transfer to a roasting pan. Cook in a preheated oven, 350°F, for about 15 minutes or until golden.

Spread the soft goats cheese over 2 slices of walnut bread. Top with the roasted asparagus spears and arrange the sliced firm goats cheese over them.

Sprinkle with the lemon thyme, top with the remaining slices of bread, and toast in a sandwich grill for 3–4 minutes or according to the manufacturer's instructions until the bread is golden and the cheese has melted. Serve with a drizzle of truffle oil.

For cheese, bacon, & maple syrup panini, spread 3 tablespoons cream cheese over 2 slices of walnut bread. Top each with 2 slices of broiled bacon and drizzle over 1 teaspoon maple syrup. Top each with another slice of walnut bread and cook in a sandwich grill as above.

pear & gorgonzola pizzas

Makes **2**
Preparation time **10 minutes**,
  plus proving
Cooking time **20 minutes**

Pizza base

1 x ¼ oz envelope **active dry
  yeast**
1 tablespoon **skim milk
  powder**
½ teaspoon **salt**
2¾ cups **white bread flour**
1 teaspoon **superfine sugar**
1 tablespoon **olive oil**
¾ cup hand-hot **water**

Topping

1 teaspoon **olive oil**
2 small **pears** peeled, cored,
  and cut into 16 slices
4 oz **Gorgonzola cheese**,
  roughly crumbled
handful **arugula**, to garnish

Mix together the yeast, milk powder, salt, flour, and sugar in a large bowl. Stir the oil into the water and pour onto the flour mixture. Mix to form a soft dough, adding a little extra water or flour if necessary.

Knead on a lightly floured surface for 5 minutes. Transfer to a lightly oiled bowl, cover with a damp cloth, and allow to prove in a warm place until the dough has doubled in size.

Divide the dough in 2 and knead each ball. Roll into a circle about 8 inches across and place on a baking sheet. Brush the dough with 1 teaspoon oil, then layer over the pear slices and sprinkle with the Gorgonzola cheese.

Cook in a preheated oven, 425°F, for 15–20 minutes until golden and bubbling and the dough is browned. Serve immediately with a green salad, if desired.

For Gorgonzola, prosciutto, & arugula pizzas, prepare the pizza bases as above. Heat 1 tablespoon olive oil in a skillet and cook 1 sliced onion until softened. Arrange on the pizza bases, sprinkle with the Gorgonzola and cook as above. Tear 6 slices of prosciutto into pieces and lay them over the pizzas, top with a handful of arugula and a drizzle of olive oil, and serve.

quick
suppers

tomato, olive, & feta tartlets

Serves **2**
Preparation time **10 minutes**
Cooking time **15 minutes**

6 oz **puff pastry**, thawed if
  frozen
8 **cherry tomatoes**, halved
12 pitted **olives**, halved
3 oz **feta cheese**, crumbled
2 teaspoons **olive oil**

Pesto
large handful of **basil** leaves
1 tablespoon toasted **pine
  nuts**
1 tablespoon grated
  Parmesan cheese
1 small **garlic clove**, chopped
2 tablespoons **olive oil**
salt and **black pepper**

Divide the pastry in 2 and roll each piece into a square
about 6 x 6 inches. With a knife, lightly mark a border
around each pastry square about ½ inch in from the
edge and transfer to a baking sheet.

Make the pesto. Put the basil, pine nuts, Parmesan,
garlic, and oil in a blender or food processor. Season
to taste with salt and process until combined but still
retaining some texture. (Any leftover pesto can be
stored in the refrigerator for a couple of days.)

Mix together the tomatoes, olives, feta, and oil, season
well and spread over the pastry squares, keeping within
the border.

Drizzle 2 teaspoons pesto over the tartlets and bake
in a preheated oven, 425°F, for about 15 minutes until
golden and puffed up. Serve with a crisp green salad,
if desired.

For pepper & Brie tartlets, prepare the pastry
squares as above. Spread 1 teaspoon pesto over
each, then place 1 roasted skinned and sliced red bell
pepper within the border and top each with 2 slices of
Brie. Sprinkle with a little fresh chopped oregano and
a drizzle of olive oil and cook as above.

ricotta & prosciutto pasta

Serves **2**
Preparation time **10 minutes**
Cooking time **15 minutes**

6 oz **pasta shapes**
1 tablespoon **olive oil**
1 small **onion**, finely chopped
1 **garlic clove**, crushed
3 oz **prosciutto**, torn into bite-size pieces
½ cup **ricotta cheese**
2 cups **arugula**
2 tablespoons grated **Parmesan cheese**
2 tablespoons **white wine**
salt and **black pepper**

Cook the pasta in boiling water according to the instructions on the package. Drain.

Meanwhile, heat the oil in a nonstick skillet, add the onion and garlic, and fry for 3 minutes until softened. Then add the ham and cook for 1 minute.

Add the ricotta, arugula, Parmesan, and wine to the pan and heat through for 1 minute. Toss the sauce through the cooked pasta, season to taste with salt and pepper, and serve hot.

For ricotta, prosciutto & artichoke pasta bake, cook 6 oz pasta. Cook the onion and garlic as above. Add ½ cup ricotta to the skillet with ⅔ cup drained artichoke hearts, 3 oz prosciutto, and 2 tablespoons grated Parmesan. Stir 4 tablespoons heavy cream through the pasta, mix in the contents of the skillet, then pour it all into an ovenproof dish. Mix together 4 oz chopped mozzarella and 1 cup ciabatta bread crumbs. Sprinkle the bread crumb mixture over the pasta and bake in a preheated oven, 350°F, for 10–15 minutes until golden and bubbling.

vegetable stir-fry

Serves **2**
Preparation time **10 minutes**
Cooking time **20 minutes**

1 tablespoon **olive oil** or
   canola oil
½ **onion**, diced
½ **red bell pepper**, cored,
   seeded, and diced
1 **celery stick**, sliced
1 tablespoon **light soy sauce**
1 tablespoon **tomato ketchup**
pinch of **chili powder**
2 oz **mushrooms**, trimmed
   and sliced
5 **cherry tomatoes**, halved
2 oz **snow peas** or **green
   beans**, halved if large
½ cup **bean sprouts**
1 large **carrot**, cut into batons
scallion curls, to garnish
   (optional)

Heat the oil in a large nonstick pan or wok. Add the onion and cook for 2 minutes.

Add the red pepper and celery and sauté for a few minutes. Add the soy sauce, tomato ketchup, and chili powder and stir well.

Add the remaining vegetables and stir-fry over a medium heat for 10–15 minutes until the vegetables are tender. Add a small amount of water if necessary.

Garnish the stir-fry with scallion curls (if desired) and serve with whole-wheat pita bread.

For chicken & noodle stir-fry, thinly slice 2 small boneless, skinless chicken breasts and fry them with a large diced onion. Continue as above and add 4 oz cooked noodles once the vegetables are almost tender. Sprinkle with 2 tablespoons chopped peanuts and serve.

feta, fresh herb, & arugula frittata

Serves **2**
Preparation time **5 minutes**
Cooking time **10 minutes**

4 **eggs**, beaten
2 tablespoons chopped
  herbs, such as chives,
  chervil, and parsley
1 tablespoon **heavy cream**
1 tablespoon **olive oil**
1 small **red onion**, finely sliced
½ **red bell pepper**, seeded
  and finely sliced
4 oz **feta cheese**
large handful of **arugula
  leaves**
salt and **black pepper**

Beat together the eggs, herbs, and cream.

Heat the oil in a nonstick skillet with an ovenproof handle, add the onion and pepper, and fry for 3–4 minutes until just softened. Pour in the egg mixture and cook for about 3 minutes until almost set.

Crumble over the feta, then cook under a preheated hot broiler until golden. Top with the arugula and serve.

For potato & goats cheese frittata, beat together the eggs, herbs, and cream as above. Add 4 cooked and sliced new potatoes to the egg mixture and cook as above. Arrange 4 slices of firm goats cheese over the frittata and finish cooking under a preheated hot broiler. Serve with arugula.

cabbage & anchovy pasta

Serves **2**
Preparation time **5 minutes**
Cooking time **15 minutes**

6 oz **pasta shapes**
1 tablespoon **olive oil**
¼ **Savoy cabbage**, finely
  shredded
1 **garlic clove**, sliced
4 **anchovies**, finely chopped
2 tablespoons **pine nuts**
2 tablespoons grated
  Parmesan cheese

Cook the pasta in boiling water according to the instructions on the package. Drain and keep warm.

Meanwhile, heat the oil in a skillet. Add the cabbage and garlic and cook for 5–6 minutes until the cabbage is tender. Add the anchovies, pine nuts, and Parmesan and stir to combine.

Toss the cabbage mixture through the pasta and serve immediately.

For creamy spinach pasta, cook 6 oz pasta as above. Heat 1 tablespoon olive oil and cook 3½ cups baby leaf spinach for 5–6 minutes. Omit the anchovies but instead add 2 tablespoons mascarpone and 1 tablespoon grated Parmesan to the pan. Stir the spinach mixture through the pasta and serve.

chicken with potatoes & beans

Serves **2**
Preparation time **10 minutes**,
  plus marinating
Cooking time **15 minutes**

2 boneless, skinless **chicken
  breasts**
1 tablespoon **pesto** (see
  pages 12–13 for
  homemade)
2 tablespoons **mascarpone
  cheese**

Potatoes
8 oz new **potatoes**
2 tablespoons **sour cream**
1 tablespoon **wholegrain
  mustard**
4 **scallions**, chopped

Green beans
5 oz **green beans**
1 teaspoon **olive oil**
1 tablespoon **butter**
1 **garlic clove**, crushed

Make 3 deep slashes in the top of each chicken breast
and place them in a nonmetallic dish. Mix together the
pesto and mascarpone, pour over the chicken, and
allow to marinate for 10 minutes.

Heat a griddle pan or skillet until hot and cook the
chicken breasts for 3–4 minutes on each side until
cooked through. Pour over any remaining marinade
and heat through for 1 minute.

Meanwhile, cook the potatoes in boiling salted water
until tender. Drain and toss through the sour cream,
mustard, and scallions, and gently crush with the back
of a fork.

Cook the beans in a small saucepan of boiling water
for 2 minutes and drain. Heat the oil and butter in a
skillet, add the garlic and fry for 1 minute, add the
beans and stir-fry for 1 minute. Serve the chicken with
the potatoes and beans.

For creamy pesto chicken tortillas, prepare a
marinade of 1 tablespoon pesto and 2 tablespoons
mascarpone cheese. Marinate the chicken in the
mixture for at least 10 minutes, then cook as above.
Allow to cool slightly and cut into ½ inch slices. Roll
the chicken slices in warmed flour tortillas, spoon over
any remaining marinade, and serve with plenty of fresh
green salad.

open chicken & spinach ravioli

Serves **2**
Preparation time **5 minutes**
Cooking time **10 minutes**

1 tablespoon **olive oil**
1 large **chicken breast**, thinly
  sliced
1 **garlic clove**, crushed
4¼ cups **baby leaf spinach**
⅔ cup **ricotta cheese**
good pinch of **grated nutmeg**
1 tablespoon grated
  Parmesan cheese, plus
  extra to serve
3 fresh **pasta sheets**, halved
salt and **black pepper**

Heat half the oil in a nonstick skillet, add the chicken, and fry for 2–3 minutes or until just cooked. Add the garlic and spinach and cook until the spinach is wilted and any excess liquid has evaporated.

Add the ricotta, nutmeg, and Parmesan to the pan, stir through and remove from the heat. Season to taste with salt and pepper.

Meanwhile, cook the pasta in boiling water for about 5 minutes or until just cooked. Drain. On each serving plate layer 3 pieces of pasta with the chicken mixture, finishing with a piece of pasta on top. Scatter with Parmesan, drizzle over the remaining oil and serve.

For open vegetarian ravioli, arrange a good selection of vegetables (such as cored, seeded and sliced bell peppers, sliced zucchini, mushrooms, sliced eggplant, and chopped onion) on a baking sheet. Drizzle with olive oil and sprinkle with a handful of fresh herbs. Cook in a preheated oven, 350°F, for 15–20 minutes. Layer the vegetables onto the cooked pasta sheets with 3 oz torn mozzarella. Top with the pasta sheets as above and sprinkle with some grated Parmesan before serving.

citrus chicken with rice salad

Serves **2**
Preparation time **10 minutes**,
  plus marinating
Cooking time **15 minutes**

2 boneless, skinless **chicken
  breasts**, sliced lengthwise
  into strips
2 tablespoons **buttermilk**
grated zest and juice of
  ½ **lime**
1 **garlic clove**, crushed
pinch of **ground coriander**
1 tablespoon chopped
  cilantro

Rice salad
½ cup **mixed basmati** and
  wild rice
1 tablespoon **olive oil**
4 **scallions**, sliced
3 tablespoons **cashew nuts**,
  roughly chopped
handful of **baby leaf spinach**
grated zest and juice of
  1 orange
1 tablespoon **soy sauce**

Put the chicken strips in a nonmetallic dish. Mix
together the buttermilk, lime zest and juice, and garlic,
pour the mixture over the chicken, turn to coat evenly,
and set aside for at least 10 minutes. Alternatively,
prepare the marinade in the morning and leave the
chicken in it in the refrigerator all day.

Cook the rice according to the instructions on the
package. Drain thoroughly.

Heat the oil in a small skillet. Fry the scallions for
1 minute. Toss the onions through the rice, and then
add the cashew nuts, spinach, orange zest and juice,
and soy sauce. Set aside.

Thread the chicken evenly on 4 skewers and cook,
turning from time to time, under a preheated hot broiler
for 4–5 minutes. Serve with the rice salad.

For angler fish & shrimp skewers, instead of the
chicken, prepare a marinade with 2 tablespoons
buttermilk, the grated zest and juice of ½ lime, a
crushed garlic clove, and a pinch of coriander.
Marinade 7 oz firm white angler fish, cut into cubes,
and 12 raw jumbo shrimp for at least 20 minutes.
Prepare the rice salad as above, before threading the
fish and shrimp onto 4 presoaked bamboo skewers
and cook, turning, under a preheated hot broiler until
the fish is cooked through.

chicken ratatouille

Serves **2**
Preparation time **20 minutes**
Cooking time **20–25 minutes**

2 tablespoons **olive oil**
2 boneless, skinless **chicken breasts**, each about 5 oz, cut into 1 inch pieces
2 tablespoons **zucchini**, thinly sliced
½ cup **eggplant**, cubed
1 **onion**, thinly sliced
1 small **green bell pepper**, seeded and sliced
1 cup sliced **mushrooms**
13 oz can **chopped tomatoes**
2 **garlic cloves**, finely chopped
1 teaspoon **vegetable bouillon powder**
1 teaspoon crushed dried **basil**
1 teaspoon dried **parsley**
½ teaspoon **black pepper**
fresh basil leaves, to garnish

Heat the oil in a large skillet. Add the chicken and cook, stirring, for about 2 minutes. Add the zucchini, eggplant, onion, green bell pepper, and mushrooms. Cook, stirring occasionally, for about 15 minutes, or until tender.

Add the tomatoes to the pan, stirring gently. Stir in the garlic, vegetable bouillon powder, basil, parsley, and pepper and simmer, uncovered, for about 5 minutes or until a fork goes easily into the chicken.

Serve garnished with the fresh basil leaves.

For stuffed ratatouille peppers, make the ratatouille as above but omit the chicken. Halve, core and seed 2 red bell peppers and place them in an ovenproof dish. Spoon the ratatouille into the pepper halves and sprinkle over 4 oz chopped mozzarella cheese. Cook in a preheated oven, 350°F, for 20 minutes or until the peppers are tender.

shish kebabs & tzatziki pitas

Serves **2**
Preparation time **10 minutes**
Cooking time **5 minutes**

8 oz **ground lamb**
½ teaspoon **ground cumin**
½ teaspoon **ground
  coriander**
2 tablespoons roughly
  chopped **cilantro**
1 **garlic clove**, halved
½ small **onion**, roughly
  chopped

Tzatziki
4 tablespoons **Greek** or
  whole milk yogurt
1 **garlic clove**, crushed
¼ **cucumber**, finely chopped
1 tablespoon chopped
  parsley

Make the tzatziki. Mix together the yogurt, crushed garlic, cucumber, and chopped parsley, transfer to a small bowl, and set aside.

Put the lamb, cumin, coriander, cilantro, garlic, and onion in a food processor and blend until well combined but still retaining a little texture.

Divide the mixture into 4 and use damp hands to shape it around 4 metal or presoaked bamboo skewers. Cook under a preheated hot broiler for 3–4 minutes, turning regularly until browned and the lamb is just cooked through.

Serve 2 kebabs in a toasted pita bread with crisp green salad and a spoonful of tzatziki.

For pork burgers & tzatziki rolls, combine in a food processor 8 oz ground pork with ½ teaspoon each ground cumin and ground coriander, 2 tablespoons chopped cilantro, a garlic clove, and ½ small onion. Process briefly so that the mixture retains some texture. Divide the mixture in half and shape it into 2 burgers. Cook the burgers on a preheated hot griddle for 2–3 minutes on each side and serve in a toasted roll with salad and a spoonful of tzatziki.

smoked haddock fishcakes

Serves **2**

Preparation time **10 minutes**,
  plus chilling

Cooking time **40 minutes**

7 oz **smoked haddock**,
  skinned

¾ cup **milk**

2 **scallions**, sliced

1 tablespoon **mayonnaise**

1 tablespoon chopped **dill
  weed**, plus extra sprigs to
  garnish

1¾ cups cooked mashed
  potato

vegetable oil, for frying

To coat

1 tablespoon **seasoned flour**

1 **egg**, beaten

2 cups fresh **bread crumbs**

Potato wedges

2 large **potatoes**, cut into
  wedges and parboiled

1 tablespoon **olive oil**

3 **garlic cloves** with skin on

salt and **black pepper**

Put the fish in a saucepan, pour over the milk, and simmer for 5 minutes. Discard the milk and flake the fish from the skin. Mix together in a bowl the flaked fish with the scallions, mayonnaise, dill, and mashed potato.

Shape the mixture into 4 patties. Dip each fishcake in the seasoned flour, then in egg and finally in breadcrumbs, ensuring that they are all evenly coated. Chill for least 30 minutes.

Put the parboiled potato wedges in a baking pan with the oil and garlic. Season with salt and pepper. Cook in a preheated oven, 400°F, for 30–40 minutes until golden.

Heat a little oil in a skillet and fry the fishcakes for 1–2 minutes on each side until golden. Serve garnished with the sprigs of dill, with the potato wedges and a good squeeze of lemon.

For crab cakes, heat 1 tablespoon olive oil in a skillet. Fry ½ chopped onion and 1 finely chopped green bell pepper for 3–4 minutes and add 1 crushed garlic clove and 2–3 finely chopped scallions. Fry for 3–4 minutes more and tip into a bowl. Mix 1 cup bread crumbs with 4 oz white and brown crabmeat, 1 tablespoon Worcestershire sauce, a good pinch of cayenne pepper, 1–2 tablespoons chopped parsley, and a lightly beaten egg. Season with salt. Mix with the onion mixture and shape into 2 balls. Flatten them between your hands to make 2 cakes. Heat a little sunflower oil in a skillet and fry the cakes for 4–5 minutes on each side.

parmesan & cornmeal flounder

Serves **2**
Preparation time **10 minutes**
Cooking time **10 minutes**

2 skinned **flounder fillets**
1 **egg**, beaten
2 tablespoons **cornmeal**
2 tablespoons grated
  Parmesan cheese
pinch of **cayenne pepper**
vegetable oil, for frying

Tartare sauce
1 tablespoon **mayonnaise**
1 tablespoon **sour cream**
1 **gherkin**, finely chopped
1 tablespoon **capers**, rinsed
  and roughly chopped
1 teaspoon chopped **dill
  weed**
grated zest and juice of
  ½ **lime**

Make the tartare sauce. In a small bowl mix together the mayonnaise, sour cream, gherkin, capers, dill, and lime zest and juice.

Cut the flounder into strips and dip each strip in the beaten egg. Mix together the cornmeal, Parmesan, and cayenne, and coat the fish strips evenly in the mixture.

Heat a little oil in a skillet. Add the flounder strips, in batches if necessary, and fry for 2–3 minutes, turning occasionally to prevent burning.

Serve the goujons in a soft roll with salad and a spoonful of tartare sauce.

For Parmesan-crusted chicken with sweet potato fries, peel 2 large sweet potatoes and cut the flesh into thick fries. Toss the fries in 1 tablespoon olive oil, sprinkle over a pinch of cayenne pepper and a little salt, and roast in a preheated oven, 400°F, for 30 minutes, then toss together with a handful of fresh chopped herbs. Cut 2 skinless chicken fillets into strips and coat them in beaten egg and the cornmeal, Parmesan, and cayenne mix. Heat some vegetable oil in a skillet and cook the chicken strips for 4–5 minutes. Serve the chicken with the sweet potato fries and a green salad.

arugula pesto mussels

Serves **2**

Preparation time **20 minutes**,
  plus preparing the mussels

Cooking time **15–20 minutes**

2 lb **mussels**, scrubbed and
  debearded

2 tablespoons **arugula pesto**
  (see below for homemade)

Lemon bread crumbs

about 1½ oz small, stale
  baguette or other crusty
  bread

finely grated zest of ½ **lemon**

1 **garlic clove**, finely chopped

1 tablespoon **olive oil**

1 tablespoon chopped **flat-
  leaf parsley**

¼ teaspoon **dried red pepper
  flakes** (optional)

Prepare the bread crumbs. Put the bread in a clean, dry food processor and process into crumbs. Add the lemon zest, garlic, oil, parsley, and pepper flakes (if using) and mix well.

Heat a nonstick skillet over a low heat and add the bread crumb mixture. Toast gently for about 5 minutes, stirring frequently to prevent burning, until crisp and golden. Transfer the bread crumbs to a plate lined with paper towels to absorb any excess oil and allow to cool.

Mix the dry mussels with the pesto sauce in a dry bowl until thoroughly coated, then divide between 2 large pieces of foil. Fold up the edges and scrunch them together to seal. Heat a griddle pan over a medium heat, put the foil parcels directly on the griddle and cook for 15–20 minutes until the mussels have opened. Discard any that remain closed.

Put the foil parcels in warm bowls. Diners open the parcels themselves and sprinkle the crispy bread crumbs over the mussels and add more pesto to taste. Serve with cooked asparagus tips and plenty of crusty bread.

For homemade arugula pesto, to mix with the mussels, put 10 oz roughly chopped arugula, 1 small finely chopped garlic clove, 5 tablespoons olive oil, and 1½ tablespoons lightly toasted pine nuts in a food processor or blender and process until fairly smooth. Pour into a bowl and stir in 1 tablespoon grated Parmesan cheese, 1 tablespoon lemon juice, and 3 tablespoons sour cream. Season to taste with salt and pepper. These quantities make 1¼ cups.

sweet potato & roquefort toasts

Serves **2**
Preparation time **5 minutes**
Cooking time **12 minutes**

3 tablespoons **honey**
1 teaspoon dried **red pepper flakes**
3 tablespoons **sesame oil**
6 tablespoons **olive oil**
1 large **sweet potato**, peeled and thickly sliced
2 oz **sugar snap peas**
2 ready-made **potato cakes** (see below for homemade) or **pita breads**
2 oz **Roquefort cheese**
salt and **black pepper**

Mix together the honey, red pepper flakes, sesame oil, and olive oil in a small bowl. Put the sweet potato slices and sugar snap peas in a large bowl and toss them with half of the honey dressing until they are evenly coated. Season to taste with salt and pepper.

Transfer the vegetables to a baking sheet, arranging them so the potatoes are in a single layer. Cook under a preheated hot broiler for 8 minutes, turning occasionally, until the potatoes are soft and golden.

When they are cool enough to handle, arrange the potato slices and peas over one of the potato cakes and crumble the blue cheese over the top.

Top with the remaining potato cake to create a sandwich and toast in a sandwich grill for 3–4 minutes or according to the manufacturer's instructions until the potato cake is golden and the cheese is just melting. Cut in half and serve immediately with a small bowl of the remaining honey dressing to drizzle if desired.

For homemade potato cakes, mix together ¼ cup unsalted butter with 2 cups self-rising flour. Add ⅔ cup cooked mashed potato and 3–4 tablespoons milk to make a soft dough. Roll out on a lightly floured surface to about 1 inch thickness and cut into 12 rounds with a cookie cutter. Transfer to a lightly greased baking sheet and cook in a preheated oven, 400°F, for 15–18 minutes.

salmon curry with tomato salad

Serves **2**
Preparation time **10 minutes**
Cooking time **20 minutes**

1 teaspoon **vegetable oil**
1 tablespoon **butter**
1 small **onion**, sliced
1 **garlic clove**, chopped
1 teaspoon **tandoori spice mix**
1 **cinnamon stick**
10 **cherry tomatoes**, halved
4 tablespoons **sour cream**
grated zest and juice of
  ½ **lime**
7 oz skinless **salmon fillet**, cut
  into chunks
1 tablespoon chopped **mint**
1 tablespoon chopped
  cilantro

Tomato & onion salad
5 oz vine-ripened **tomatoes**,
  thinly sliced
1 small **red onion**, finely sliced
handful of **cilantro**, chopped
1 teaspoon **lemon juice**

Heat the oil and butter in a small skillet. Add the onion and garlic and fry for 2–3 minutes until softened. Stir in the spice mix and cinnamon stick and fry for a minute more. Add the tomatoes, sour cream, lime zest and juice and heat for a minute.

Put the salmon in an ovenproof dish. Spoon over the sauce, cover the dish tightly with foil, and cook in a preheated oven, 400°F, for 15–20 minutes or until the salmon is just cooked.

Meanwhile, make the salad by tossing together the tomatoes, onion, and cilantro. Dress with lemon juice.

Serve the salmon with basmati rice and the tomato and onion salad.

For paneer curry, prepare the sauce as above. Cut 5 oz paneer into cubes and put the pieces in an ovenproof dish. Pour over the sauce, making sure the paneer cubes are evenly coated, cover with foil, and cook as above. Serve with boiled rice and the tomato and onion salad.

shrimp balls & sweet chili sauce

Serves **2**
Preparation time **10 minutes**
Cooking time **5 minutes**

10 oz raw **jumbo shrimp**,
 shelled
2 **scallions**, roughly chopped
grated zest of ½ **lime**
1 tablespoon chopped
 cilantro
1 teaspoon **fish sauce**
 (nam pla)
1 tablespoon **cornstarch**
peanut oil, for frying

Sweet chili sauce
2 tablespoons **rice wine
 vinegar**
1 tablespoon **superfine sugar**
1 **red chili**, finely chopped
½ **red onion**, finely chopped
1 tablespoon chopped
 cilantro

Put the shrimp, scallions, lime zest, cilantro, and fish sauce in a food processor or blender and process for about 20 seconds until well combined but retaining a little texture.

Shape the mixture into 12 balls and lightly dust them in cornstarch. Heat a little oil in a nonstick skillet and fry the balls for 2–3 minutes until golden all over. Drain on paper towels.

Meanwhile, make the chili sauce. Put the vinegar and sugar in a small saucepan and heat gently to dissolve the sugar. Increase the heat and boil for a couple of minutes until the mixture becomes syrupy. Add the chili and red onion and allow to cool, then stir through the cilantro.

Serve the shrimp balls with the chili sauce in a bowl for dipping, and a crisp green salad, if desired.

For cod balls & sweet chili sauce, combine 10 oz skinless cod fillet (or any other firm white fish) with the scallions, lime zest, chopped cilantro, and fish sauce as above. Make 12 balls and roll them to coat lightly in cornstarch. Fry in vegetable oil and serve with the chili sauce, made as above, and steamed rice or warm pita bread.

hot haloumi with fattoush salad

Serves **2**
Preparation time **10 minutes**
Cooking time **2–4 minutes**

2 teaspoons **olive oil**
8 oz **haloumi cheese**, thickly
   sliced

Fattoush salad
1 **red bell pepper**, finely
   sliced
1 **yellow bell pepper**, finely
   sliced
½ cup chopped **cucumber**
¾ cup finely chopped
scallions
2 tablespoons chopped **flat-
   leaf parsley**
2 tablespoons chopped **mint**
2 tablespoons chopped
   cilantro

Dressing
1 teaspoon crushed **garlic**
2 tablespoons **olive oil** or
   flaxseed oil
4 tablespoons **lemon juice**
salt and **black pepper**

Heat the oil in a nonstick skillet. Add the haloumi and
fry over a medium to high heat for 1–2 minutes
on each side until golden brown. Keep warm.

Make the salad. Put the red and yellow bell peppers,
cucumber, scallions, parsley, mint, and cilantro in a bowl
and stir to combine.

Make the dressing. Mix the garlic with the oil and
lemon juice and season to taste with salt and pepper.

Pour the dressing over the salad and toss lightly to
mix. Serve with the warm haloumi.

For chicken fattoush salad, replace the haloumi
with 2 boneless, skinless chicken breasts, cut in half
horizontally. Heat 1 teaspoon olive oil in a skillet and
cook the chicken for 2 minutes on each side until
cooked through. Keep warm while you prepare the
salad and dressing. Serve the warm chicken on top
of the salad.

haddock, braised lettuce, & peas

Serves **2**
Preparation time **5 minutes**
Cooking time **10 minutes**

1 tablespoon **olive oil**
2 **haddock loins**, skinned
1 small **crisphead lettuce**,
  quartered
6 tablespoons **fish stock**
1 ⅓ cups **frozen peas**
1 tablespoon chopped **mint**
4 tablespoons **sour cream**

Heat the oil in a nonstick skillet. Add the fish and cook for a minute on each side, then add the lettuce, stock, and peas. Cover and simmer for 4 minutes.

Remove the lid and stir through the mint and sour cream. Heat through again and serve with steamed new potatoes, if desired.

For fried chicken with braised lettuce & peas, first make homemade chicken stock. Put 1 large chicken carcass, plus any trimmings and the giblets, except the liver, if available, 1 quartered onion, 1 roughly chopped celery stick, 1 bouquet garni or 3 bay leaves, and 1 teaspoon black peppercorns into a large, heavy saucepan and add 7 cups cold water and bring slowly to a boil. Reduce the heat and simmer gently for 1 ½ hours, skimming the surface from time to time if necessary. Strain the stock through a large sieve but don't squeeze the juice out of the vegetables or the stock will be cloudy. Allow the stock to cool completely, then chill. Remove any layer of fat that sets on the surface before use. These ingredients will make about 4 cups. Meanwhile, cook 2 boneless, skinless chicken breasts, each about 5 oz, in 1 tablespoon olive oil in a nonstick skillet. Add the lettuce and peas as above and 6 tablespoons chicken stock. Stir in the mint and sour cream, heat gently, and serve.

sausage & broccoli pasta

Serves **2**
Preparation time **5 minutes**
Cooking time **10–15 minutes**

6 oz **pasta shapes**
8 oz **broccoli**, cut into florets
1 tablespoon **olive oil**
4 good-quality **pork sausages**
pinch of **dried red papper flakes**
6 tablespoons **vegetable stock** (see page 94 for homemade)
2 tablespoons grated **Parmesan cheese**

Cook the pasta in boiling water according to the instructions on the package, adding the broccoli about 3 minutes before the end of the cooking time.

Meanwhile, heat the oil in a skillet. Add the sausages and fry for 4–5 minutes over a medium heat until browned all over. Remove from the pan and cut each into 4 or 5 pieces. Return to the pan, add the pepper flakes and stock and cook for an additional 2 minutes.

Drain the pasta and broccoli and toss together with the sausage mix. Serve sprinkled with the Parmesan and place under a preheated broiler for 2–3 minutes, if desired.

For Mediterranean sausage & broccoli pasta, cook the pasta as above, adding the broccoli florets 3 minutes before the end of the cooking time. Fry 5 oz sliced chorizo for about 5 minutes in 1 tablespoon olive oil, then add 6 tablespoons beef or chicken stock and the pepper flakes. Just before serving toss through 7 halved cherry tomatoes.

sausage, chorizo, & bean stew

Serves **2**
Preparation time **10 minutes**
Cooking time **25 minutes**

1 tablespoon **olive oil**
3 oz **chorizo**, chopped
1 small **onion**, sliced
1 **garlic clove**, sliced
½ teaspoon **paprika**
4 good-quality **pork
  sausages**, sliced
7 oz **cherry tomatoes**
¾ cup **beef stock**
13 oz can **cannellini beans**,
  rinsed and drained
1 tablespoon chopped
  parsley, to garnish

Garlic ciabatta

2 small, individual **ciabatta
  loaves**
3 tablespoons **butter**,
  softened
1 **garlic clove**, crushed
1 tablespoon chopped **herbs**,
  such as parsley, chives, and
  thyme
½ small **red chili**, finely
  chopped

Heat the oil in a large pan. Add the chorizo, onion, garlic, and paprika and fry for 2 minutes until the onion begins to soften. Remove from the pan and set aside.

Add the sausages to the pan and fry for 2–3 minutes until browned all over. Return the onion mixture to the pan along with the tomatoes, stock, and beans. Bring to a boil, cover, and transfer to a preheated oven, 350°F, and cook for 20 minutes.

Meanwhile, make 5 deep cuts in each ciabatta loaf. Mix together the butter, garlic, and herbs and spread into the cuts. Wrap the bread in foil and put them in the oven for 10–15 minutes before the end of the cooking time.

Sprinkle the parsley over the stew and serve with the garlic ciabatta.

For bean & potato stew, omit the chorizo and fry the onion, garlic, and paprika as above. Add the tomatoes, ¾ cup vegetable stock (see page 94 for homemade), and cannellini beans to the pan with 8 oz cooked and halved new potatoes and 4 oz halved green beans. Cook in the oven as above and serve garnished with chopped parsley.

baby leek & serrano ham gratin

Serves **2**
Preparation time **10 minutes**
Cooking time **20 minutes**

12 baby **leeks**, trimmed and
  cleaned
6 slices of **Serrano ham**
1 tablespoon **butter**
2 tablespoons **all-purpose
  flour**
1¼ cups **whole milk**
1 cup multigrain **bread
  crumbs**
2 oz **Gruyère cheese**
8 **cherry tomatoes**, halved
  (optional)

Steam the leeks for 2–3 minutes or until tender.
Cut the ham slices in half and wrap each leek in
half a piece ham. Place the leeks in the bottom of an
ovenproof dish that is just large enough to hold them.

Melt the butter in a small saucepan. Add the flour
and cook for 1 minute, stirring. Gradually add the milk,
stirring continuously, until you have a smooth sauce.
Simmer for 1 minute then pour over the leeks.

Mix together the bread crumbs and cheese and
sprinkle over the leeks. Arrange the tomatoes (if using)
on top, cut side up. Cook in a preheated oven, 400°F,
for 20 minutes until golden and bubbling.

For broccoli gratin, steam ½ cup broccoli florets.
Arrange them in the base of a small ovenproof dish.
Make the sauce as above and pour it over the
broccoli. Mix 1 cup fresh bread crumbs with
2 oz Cambozola or another creamy blue cheese.
Sprinkle over the top and cook as above.

beef & basil meatballs

Serves **2**
Preparation time **10 minutes**
Cooking time **20 minutes**

Meatballs
8 oz lean **ground beef**
1 tablespoon grated
  Parmesan cheese
1 tablespoon **pesto** (see
  pages **12–13**)
1 **egg yolk**
1 tablespoon fresh **bread
  crumbs**
1 tablespoon **olive oil**

Sauce
1 small **red onion**, chopped
1 **garlic clove**, crushed
7 oz can **chopped tomatoes**
2 tablespoons **light cream**
handful of **basil**, torn

Mix together the beef, Parmesan, pesto, egg yolk, and bread crumbs in a bowl. Roll the mixture between damp palms to make 20 balls.

Heat the oil in a skillet. Add the meatballs and cook for 2–3 minutes until browned all over. Remove from the pan and set aside on paper towels to drain.

Add the onion and garlic to the pan and fry for 2–3 minutes. Add the tomatoes, bring to a boil, and simmer for 5 minutes.

Add the meatballs to the pan with the cream and cook for 5 minutes more. Stir in the torn basil leaves.

Serve the meatballs with the sauce, accompanied by pasta and green salad, if desired.

For pork & chili meatballs, mix 8 oz lean ground pork with the Parmesan, pesto, egg yolk, and bread crumbs as above to make 20 balls. Cook as above. Make the sauce with an onion and garlic clove, chopped tomatoes and cream, and add a finely chopped, seeded green chili. Cook the sauce as above. Serve the meatballs with steamed rice and a green salad, if desired.

steak with anchovy herb butter

Serves **2**
Preparation time **10 minutes**
Cooking time **10 minutes**

2 sirloin steaks
1 teaspoon **vegetable oil**
salt and **black pepper**

Herb butter
2 tablespoons **unsalted butter**, slightly softened
3 **anchovy fillets**, drained and finely chopped
1 tablespoon chopped **herbs**, such as chives, parsley, and cilantro

Rub the steak with the oil and season to taste with salt and pepper. Heat a skillet or griddle until it is really hot and cook the steak for 2 minutes on each side or until cooked to your desire.

Mash together the butter, anchovy fillets, and herbs. Put half the flavored butter on each steak and serve with endive and Roquefort salad (see below) and new potatoes, if desired.

For endive & Roquefort salad, to serve as an accompaniment, mix together in a serving bowl 2 Belgian endive heads, broken into individual leaves, 3 oz crumbled Roquefort cheese, and 3 tablespoons toasted and roughly chopped hazelnuts. Drizzle over a little olive oil.

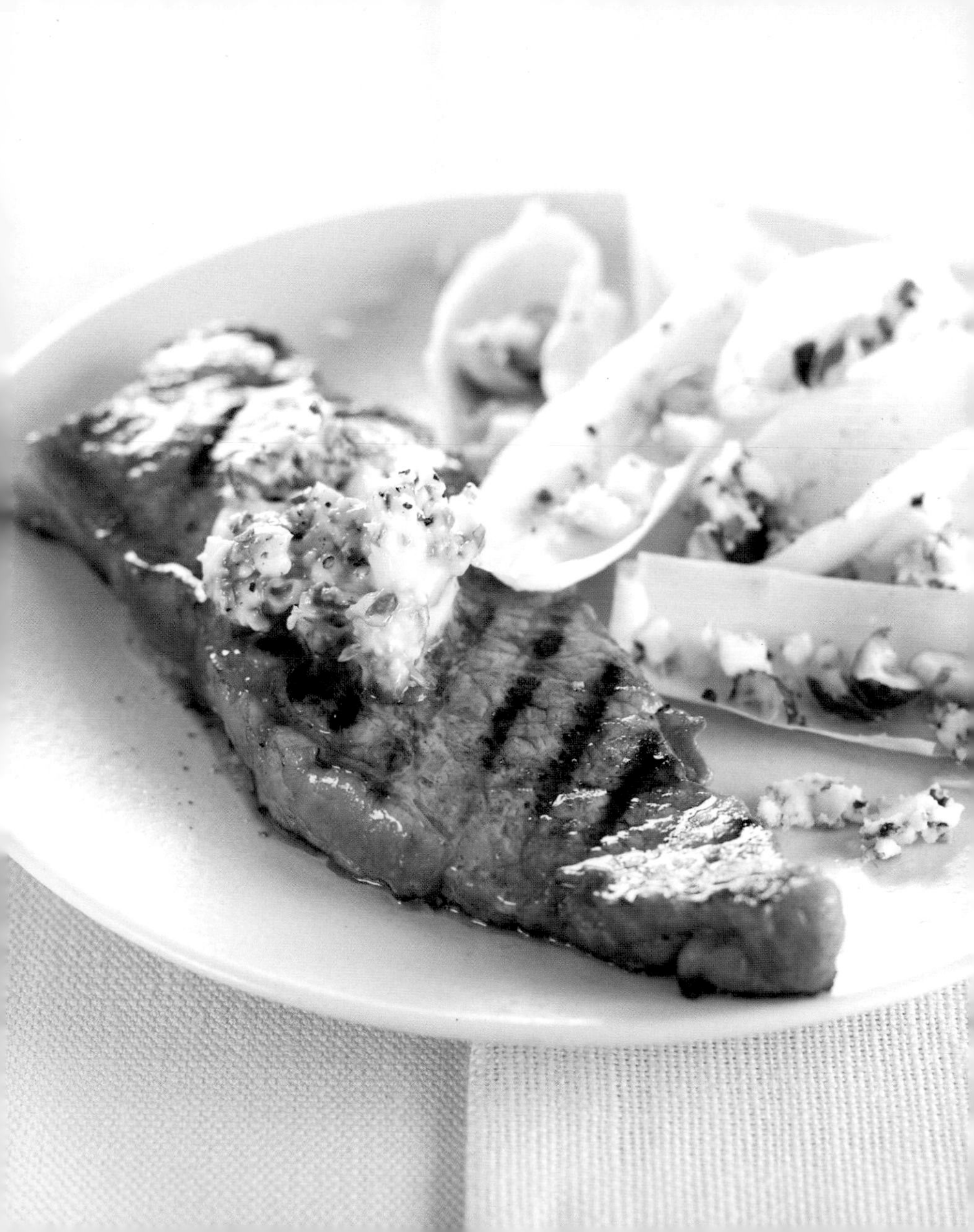

calamari with citrus & garlic mayo

Serves **2**
Preparation time **10 minutes**
Cooking time **10 minutes**

2 tablespoons **all-purpose flour**
large pinch of **dried red pepper flakes**
8 **calamari** tubes, cut into rings
vegetable oil, for deep-frying
1 tablespoon **lemon juice**

Citrus & garlic mayonnaise
1 **garlic clove**, crushed
1 **egg yolk**
6 tablespoons **olive oil**
finely grated zest and juice of ½ **lime** or **lemon**
1 tablespoon chopped **herbs**, such as cilantro and parsley

Make the citrus and garlic mayonnaise. Put the garlic, egg yolk, and lime or lemon juice and zest in a food processor or blender, process, and then gradually pour in the oil, while still blending, to give a thick mayonnaise. Stir through the herbs.

Mix together the flour and pepper flakes and coat the calamari. Heat a little oil in a skillet. Add the calamari and fry in batches until golden. Toss with the lemon juice. Serve the calamari with spoonfuls of the mayonnaise and a green salad, if desired.

For garlic shrimp with citrus & garlic mayo,
mix together 1 crushed garlic clove, ½ teaspoon paprika, ½ red chili, seeded and finely chopped, 1 tablespoon olive oil, and a little salt in a large bowl. Add 8 oz large whole raw shrimp. Heat a large, nonstick skillet and cook the shrimp, in a single layer, for 2–3 minutes. Turn and cook for 1–2 minutes more. Transfer to a warm dish and serve with the citrus and garlic mayo (above).

special
occasions

lamb burger & roasted tomatoes

Serves **2**
Preparation time **12 minutes**,
  plus chilling
Cooking time 1¼ **hours**

9 oz good-quality coarsely
  ground lamb
¼ cup ready-to-eat **dried
  apricots**, finely chopped
1–2 tablespoons finely
  chopped **cilantro**
1 tablespoon finely chopped
  flat-leaf parsley
1 **garlic clove**, crushed
1 teaspoon **ground cumin**
large pinch of **cayenne
  pepper**
large pinch of **turmeric**
salt and **black pepper**

Roasted tomatoes
3 medium **plum tomatoes**,
  halved
large pinch of **paprika**
1 **garlic clove**, chopped
2 teaspoons **olive oil**

To serve
2 **soft rolls**
salad leaves

Arrange the tomatoes, cut side up, on a lightly greased nonstick baking sheet. Sprinkle with the paprika and chopped garlic and season well with salt and pepper. Drizzle with olive oil and roast in a preheated oven, 300°F, for 1 hour. Remove and set aside until needed.

Mix the lamb, apricots, herbs, and spices in a large bowl and season well with salt and pepper. Divide the mixture in half and form them into 2 balls. Flatten into burgers. Cover and chill for 30 minutes.

Heat a griddle pan or barbecue until very hot. Brush the burgers with a little oil and cook them for 5 minutes on each side, depending on how well done you like them.

Toast the halved rolls on a hot griddle pan or barbecue and top each base with salad leaves and a burger. Put 3 roasted tomatoes on each burger and top with the lid of the roll.

For mozzarella lamb burgers, prepare 9 oz ground lamb as above, but when you have divided the mixture into 2, flatten each portion. Shape each around ½ oz mozzarella cheese and 3 fresh cilantro leaves. Smooth the meat into a burger shape and cook and serve as above.

shrimp, pea, & lemon risotto

Serves **2**
Preparation time **10 minutes**
Cooking time **20 minutes**

1 teaspoon **olive oil**
½ small **onion**, finely chopped
1 **garlic clove**, finely chopped
½ cup **risotto rice**
1 tablespoon **white wine**
1¾ cups hot **fish stock**
grated zest and juice of
  ½ **lemon**
8 oz cooked **jumbo shrimp**
1 cup **frozen peas**
1 tablespoon **butter**
2 tablespoons grated
  Parmesan cheese
1 tablespoon chopped
  parsley
salt and **black pepper**

Heat the oil in a skillet. Add the onion and garlic and fry for 2–3 minutes until softened. Add the rice and cook for a minute more, making sure that the rice is coated in the oil. Add the wine and cook for another minute, and then gradually add the stock, ladle by ladle, stirring continuously and allowing each addition of stock to be absorbed before adding the next.

Add the shrimp and peas with the final ladleful of stock and add the lemon zest and juice. Stir until the shrimp and peas are cooked and heated through. Remove the pan from the heat and stir through the butter, Parmesan, and parsley. Season to taste with salt and pepper and serve.

For broccoli & bean risotto, cook the onion, garlic, and rice as above, adding 1 tablespoon white wine and 1¾ cups vegetable stock (see page 94 for homemade). When the stock has been absorbed add ½ cup small broccoli florets and ¼ cup frozen fava beans. When the broccoli and beans are cooked, after about 4–5 minutes, remove the risotto from the heat and stir through 1 tablespoon butter, 2 tablespoons grated Parmesan, and 1 tablespoon chopped flat-leaf parsley.

baked lemon sole & asparagus

Serves **2**
Preparation time **10 minutes**
Cooking time **20 minutes**

1 tablespoon **unsalted butter**, softened
1 tablespoon chopped **herbs**, such as parsley, thyme, and chives
4 skinned **lemon sole fillets**
4 **scallions**, shredded
1 **carrot**, cut into matchsticks
1 tablespoon **white wine**
finely grated zest of ½ **lemon**
salt and **black pepper**

Pan-fried asparagus
1 tablespoon **unsalted butter**
1–2 teaspoons **olive oil**
4 oz **asparagus spears**
Parmesan cheese shavings

Mix together the butter and herbs and spread onto one side of each of the sole fillets. Roll up the fish with the herb butter on the inside.

Cut 4 squares of parchment paper, each about 10 x 10 inches. Put the scallions and carrot in the center of 2 of the pieces of parchment and top each with 2 of the sole rolls. Drizzle over the wine and sprinkle with the lemon zest. Season with salt and pepper. Put the other pieces of parchment paper on top and tightly roll up each side to make 2 parcels.

Transfer the parcels to a baking sheet and bake in a preheated oven, 400°F, for about 20 minutes.

Meanwhile, cook the asparagus. Heat the butter and oil in a skillet. Add the asparagus and fry for 2–3 minutes until just tender. Season to taste. Arrange the asparagus on warm serving plates and sprinkle with some Parmesan shavings. Add the fish parcels and serve.

For asparagus with tarragon & lemon dressing,
make the dressing by mixing together 1 tablespoon tarragon vinegar, grated zest of ½ lemon, ¼ teaspoon Dijon mustard, a pinch of sugar, 1 tablespoon chopped tarragon, and 2–3 tablespoons olive oil. Season to taste with salt and pepper. Heat 1 tablespoon olive oil in a skillet. Add 8 oz trimmed asparagus and cook for about 5 minutes, turning occasionally. Transfer to a shallow dish, pour over the dressing, and allow to stand for 5 minutes.

asian gingered salmon

Serves **2**
Preparation time **10 minutes**
Cooking time **6–10 minutes**

3–4 **scallions**, shredded
½ inch piece of **fresh ginger root**, peeled and cut into strips
1 tablespoon **dry ginger ale** or **ginger cordial**
1 tablespoon **light soy sauce**
2 skinless **salmon fillets**, each about 4 oz

Mix the scallions, fresh ginger, ginger ale or cordial, and soy sauce in a bowl.

Put the salmon in a covered skillet and poach in the mixture for 3–5 minutes on each side. Top up with a little water if needed.

Garnish the salmon with the scallions and ginger and pour over the remaining ginger ale mixture. Serve with steamed cabbage, snow peas, and new potatoes, boiled in their skins.

For creamy peppered salmon, press 2 skinless salmon fillets into 1 tablespoon crushed peppercorns. Heat 1 tablespoon olive oil in a skillet and cook the salmon for 2 minutes on each side until just cooked through. Add 4 tablespoons sour cream to the pan, cook gently to warm through, and serve with new potatoes and steamed green vegetables.

pork with apricot & sage stuffing

Serves **2**
Preparation time **10 minutes**
Cooking time **20 minutes**

10 oz **pork tenderloin**
1 tablespoon **olive oil**
1 small **onion**, finely sliced
6 ready-to-eat **dried apricots**,
  finely chopped
1 tablespoon **sage**, chopped
1 tablespoon **pine nuts**
fresh sage leaves, to garnish

Smashed beans
13 oz can **cannellini beans**,
  rinsed and drained
1 **garlic clove**, sliced
6 tablespoons **chicken stock**
  (see page 146 for
  homemade)
2 tablespoons **sour cream**
salt and **black pepper**

Make a cut along the length of the tenderloin, taking care that you do not cut all the way through.

Heat half the oil in a nonstick pan. Add the onion and fry for 2–3 minutes until softened. Add the apricots, sage, and pine nuts and cook for a minute more.

Spread the stuffing mixture along the length of the pork and secure with toothpicks or string.

Heat the remaining oil in a skillet. Add the pork and fry for a few minutes until browned all over. Transfer it to a roasting pan and cook in a preheated oven, 400°F, for 10–15 minutes or until just cooked through.

Meanwhile, put the beans, garlic, and stock in a pan and simmer for 5 minutes. Add the sour cream and season to taste with salt and pepper. Mash the bean mixture with a potato masher and serve with the pork, garnished with the whole sage leaves.

For pork tenderloin with apricots, cut 12 oz pork tenderloin into 6 slices. Cook the pork in a hot griddle pan for 7–8 minutes, transfer to an ovenproof dish, and keep warm. Cut 1 red onion into wedges, keeping the root end intact. Cook on the griddle for about 5 minutes and add to the pork. Halve and pit 4 apricots and cook the halves on the griddle for 5 minutes on each side, adding a sprig of thyme for the last minute. Add the apricots and thyme to the pork. Mix together 2 tablespoons olive oil and 2 teaspoons cider vinegar and drizzle over the pork. Serve with boiled rice.

beef tenderloin with walnut pesto

Serves **2**
Preparation time **5 minutes**
Cooking time **5 minutes**

2 pieces of **beef tenderloin**,
    each about **7** oz
½ cup **toasted walnuts**
3 tablespoons chopped mixed
    herbs, such as cilantro,
    parsley, and basil
2 tablespoons grated
    Parmesan cheese
1 **garlic clove**
2 tablespoons **olive oil**
salt and **black pepper**

Heat a griddle or heavy skillet. Season the meat with salt and pepper, add to the pan, and cook for 2 minutes on each side or until cooked to your desire.

Meanwhile, place the walnuts, herbs, Parmesan, garlic, and oil in a food processor or blender and process until combined but still retaining a little texture.

Serve the cooked steaks with the sauce spooned on top and accompanied with steamed new potatoes and sugar snap peas.

For grilled vegetables with walnut pesto, make the walnut pesto as above. Heat a griddle pan and cook a halved and seeded red bell pepper, a halved eggplant, 2 quartered red onions, and 6 asparagus spears. Serve the vegetables on a bed of steamed couscous with the pesto.

stuffed mushrooms with tofu

Serves **2**
Preparation time **15 minutes**
Cooking time **18–20 minutes**

2½ cups **boiling water**
2 teaspoons **vegetable bouillon powder**
4 large **portobello mushrooms**, stalks removed
2 tablespoons **olive oil**
¼ cup finely chopped **red onion**
2 tablespoons **pine nuts**
8 oz **tofu**, diced
½ teaspoon **cayenne pepper**
2 tablespoons chopped **basil**
½ cup finely grated **Parmesan cheese**
3½ cups **baby spinach leaves**
salt and **black pepper**

Pour the boiling water into a wide pan, then stir in the bouillon powder. Add the mushrooms, poach for 2–3 minutes, then remove and drain on paper towels.

Heat a little of the oil in a skillet. Add the onion and fry gently until soft. Remove from the heat and allow to cool.

Dry-fry the pine nuts in a clean pan until golden brown, remove from the heat, then combine with the onion, tofu, cayenne pepper, basil, and remaining oil. Season to taste with salt and black pepper.

Sprinkle some grated Parmesan over each mushroom, then stuff the onion mixture into the mushrooms. Put them in a flameproof dish about 6 inches square below a preheated medium broiler for about 10 minutes, until heated through and the cheese has melted.

Sprinkle the spinach leaves on 2 plates and arrange two hot mushrooms on top (the heat of the mushrooms will wilt the spinach).

For tofu & mushroom pasta, cook 10 oz pasta in boiling water according to the instructions on the package. Drain thoroughly. Meanwhile, slice 2 portobello mushrooms. Heat 1 tablespoon olive oil in a skillet and fry the mushrooms with 2 tablespoons chopped red onion. Add the mushrooms and onion to the pasta and add all the remaining ingredients above. Stir through 3 tablespoons heavy cream, warm gently, and serve.

moroccan lamb with couscous

Serves **2**
Preparation time **10 minutes**,
  plus marinating
Cooking time **5 minutes**

4 **lamb chops** or 2 **lamb
  steaks**
2 teaspoons **ras el hanout**
grated zest and juice of
  ½ **lemon**
1 **garlic clove**, crushed
1 tablespoon **olive oil**

Couscous
1¼ cups boiling **chicken
  stock** (see page 146 for
  homemade)
¾ cup **couscous**
4 fresh or ready-to-eat dried
  apricots, chopped
⅓ cup blanched and toasted
  almonds, roughly chopped
2 tablespoons chopped
  cilantro
salt and **black pepper**

Put the lamb in a nonmetallic dish. Mix together the ras
el hanout, lemon zest and juice, garlic, and oil. Season
to taste with salt and pepper and rub the mixture all
over the lamb. Allow to marinate for at least 1 hour.

Cook the lamb under a preheated hot broiler, turning
once, for about 2 minutes each side, until it is browned
and cooked to your desire.

Meanwhile, pour the boiling stock over the couscous,
cover tightly, and allow to absorb the liquid for 5 minutes.
Fluff it up with a fork.

Toss the apricots and cilantro through the couscous
and serve with the lamb.

For couscous with broiled vegetables, mix ¾ cup
couscous with 1¼ cups boiling vegetable stock.
Chop 1 red bell pepper and ½ yellow bell pepper.
Halve 3 small zucchini and cut 1 red onion into
wedges. Put the vegetables in a roasting pan with
12 cherry tomatoes and 1 sliced garlic clove. Drizzle
over 1 tablespoon olive oil and cook under a preheated
hot broiler, turning occasionally, for 5–6 minutes.
Add 2 oz trimmed asparagus to the pan and cook
for 2–3 minutes more. Fork the grated zest and juice
of ½ lemon through the couscous and serve with
the vegetables.

stilton soufflés

Serves **2**
Preparation time **10 minutes**
Cooking time **15 minutes**

1 tablespoon **butter**, plus
  extra for greasing
1 tablespoon grated
  Parmesan cheese
2 tablespoons **all-purpose**
  flour
6 tablespoons **milk**
2 oz **Stilton cheese**, crumbled
1 **egg**, separated

Butter 2 ramekins, each holding ⅔ cup, and coat the bottom and sides with grated Parmesan.

Melt the butter in a small saucepan and add the flour. Beat to make a smooth paste, then gradually add the milk, stirring all the time, until the sauce thickens. Allow to cool a little, then beat in the Stilton and egg yolk.

Beat the egg white in a clean bowl until it forms soft peaks. Fold into the cheese mixture, then spoon into the prepared ramekins. Cook in a preheated oven, 400°F, for about 15 minutes until golden and risen. Serve hot with watercress salad (see below) and some crusty, seeded bread.

For watercress & apple salad, to serve as an accompaniment, mix together in a small bowl 2 tablespoons lemon juice, ½ teaspoon Dijon mustard, 1 teaspoon honey, and 1 tablespoon olive oil. Finely slice 1 apple and mix with 1¼ cups watercress. Drizzle the dressing over the watercress and apple, toss, and serve.

eggplant parcels with pine nuts

Serves **2**

Preparation time **30 minutes**,
   plus chilling

Cooking time **12–15 minutes**

1 tablespoon **pine nuts**
1 long, large **eggplant**
4 oz **mozzarella cheese**
1 large or 2 small **plum
   tomatoes**
8 large **basil leaves**, plus
   extra, torn, to garnish
1 tablespoon **olive oil**
salt and **black pepper**

Tomato dressing
2 tablespoons **olive oil**
1 teaspoon **balsamic vinegar**
1 teaspoon **sundried tomato
   paste**
1 teaspoon **lemon juice**

Make the dressing. Beat together the oil, vinegar, tomato paste, and lemon juice in a small bowl. Set aside.

Dry-fry the pine nuts in a hot pan until golden brown. Set aside.

Cut the stalk off the eggplant and cut it lengthwise to give 8 slices (disregarding the ends). Put the slices in a pan of boiling salted water and cook for 2 minutes. Drain and dry on paper towels. Cut the mozzarella into 4 slices and the tomato into 8 slices (disregarding the outer edges).

Put 2 eggplant slices in an ovenproof dish, forming an X-shape. Put a slice of tomato on top, season with salt and pepper, add a basil leaf, a slice of mozzarella, another basil leaf, then more salt and pepper, and finally another slice of tomato. Fold the edges of the eggplant around the filling to make a parcel. Repeat with the other ingredients to make 4 parcels in total. Cover and chill in the refrigerator for 20 minutes.

Brush the eggplant parcels with oil. Put the dish under a preheated hot broiler and cook for about 5 minutes on each side until golden brown. Serve 2 parcels per person, drizzled with the dressing, and sprinkled with the pine nuts and torn basil leaves.

For eggplant parcels with garlic bruschetta, drizzle 4 slices of ciabatta with 1 tablespoon olive oil and rub with garlic. Toast until golden. Make eggplant parcels as above and place one on each slice, top with Parmesan shavings, and sprinkle with 1 tablespoon toasted pine nuts.

smoked salmon & veg pasta

Serves **2**
Preparation time **10 minutes**
Cooking time **30 minutes**

1 **zucchini**, chopped
1 **red bell pepper**, cored,
   seeded, and chopped
1 **red onion**, cut into thin
   wedges
2 **garlic cloves**, sliced
2 tablespoons **olive oil**
5 oz **pasta shapes**
5 oz **smoked salmon**
6 tablespoons **heavy cream**
grated zest and juice of
   ½ **lemon**
1 tablespoon **toasted**
   pine nuts
handful of **basil leaves**, torn

Put the zucchini, red bell pepper, red onion, and garlic in a roasting pan, drizzle over the oil, and cook in a preheated oven, 425°F, for 25–30 minutes until the vegetables are tender and beginning to char.

Meanwhile, cook the pasta in boiling water according to the instructions on the package. Drain.

Cut the salmon into bite-size pieces and mix with the cream, lemon zest and juice, pine nuts, and torn basil leaves. Toss the cream sauce through the pasta, add the roasted vegetables, and warm through gently before serving.

For feta & chorizo roasted vegetable pasta, add 3 oz sliced chorizo to the vegetables halfway through the cooking time and replace the salmon with 2 oz crumbled feta cheese. Then toss the cream sauce through the pasta with the roasted vegetables, warming gently before serving.

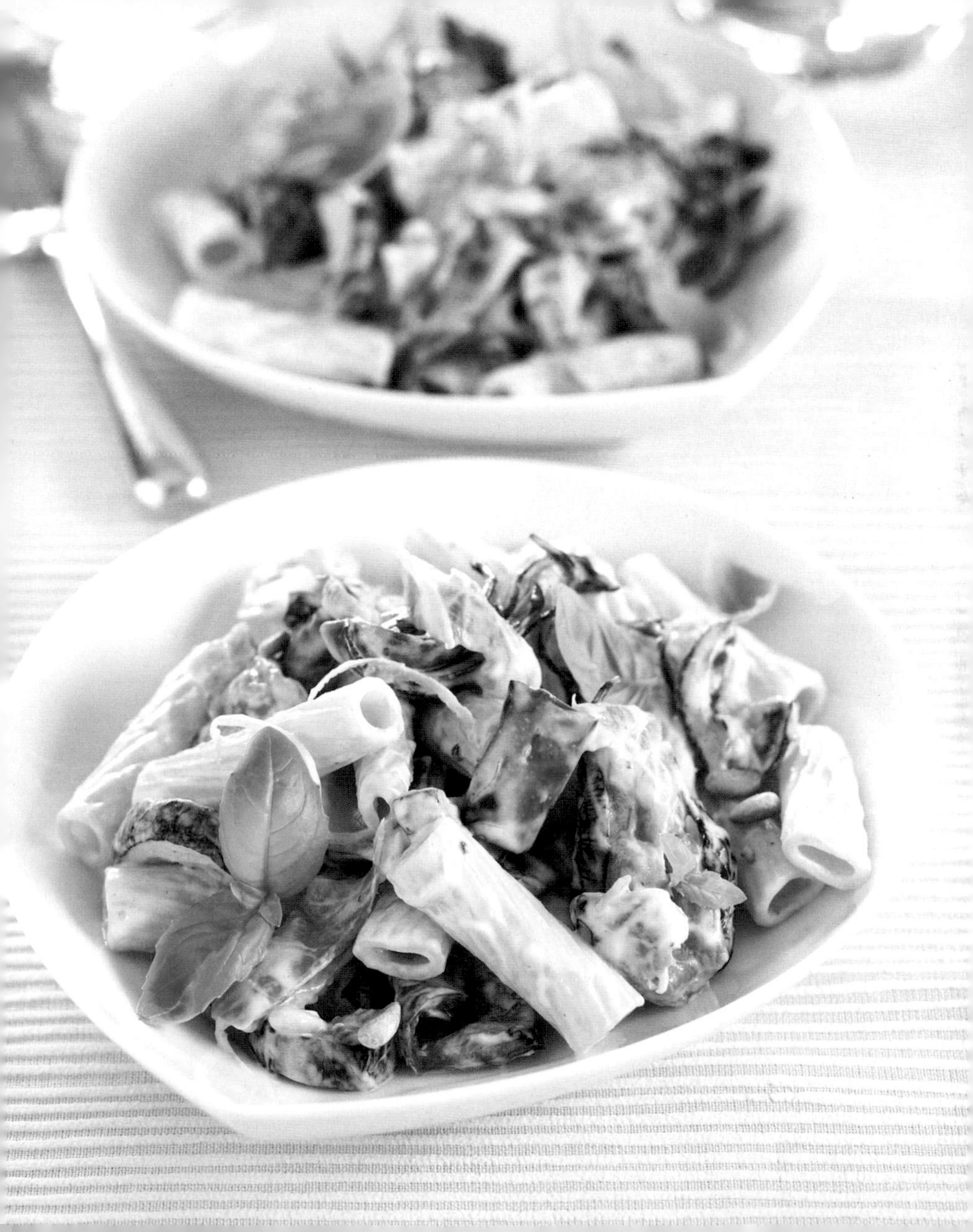

tarragon chicken with potatoes

Serves **2**

Preparation time **10 minutes**, plus marinating

Cooking time **1 hour**

2 **chicken breasts**, each cut into about 8 slices

4 tablespoons **lemon juice**

1 **garlic clove**, crushed

handful of **tarragon**, chopped

2 tablespoons **butter**

4 oz mixed **mushrooms**, sliced

¾ cup **heavy cream**

salt and **black pepper**

Sliced potatoes

3 large unpeeled **potatoes**, thinly sliced

1 teaspoon finely chopped **thyme**

1 tablespoon **olive oil**

⅔ cup **vegetable stock** (see page 94 for homemade)

½ tablespoon **butter**

Layer the potato slices and thyme in a well-greased, ovenproof dish. Mix together the oil and stock and pour over the potatoes. Dot over the butter, cover with foil, and bake in a preheated oven, 325°F, for 1 hour, removing the foil halfway through cooking.

Meanwhile, put the chicken in a nonmetallic dish. Mix together the lemon juice, garlic, and tarragon, pour the mixture over the chicken, and allow to marinate for 30 minutes.

Heat the butter in a skillet and fry the mushrooms, then add the chicken and any juices and fry for an additional 3 minutes. Add the cream to the pan and season with salt and pepper. Simmer gently for a couple of minutes until the chicken is just cooked. Serve with the potatoes and steamed green beans.

For tarragon chicken & mushroom pasta, cook 5 oz pasta shapes in boiling water according to the instructions on the package. Drain thoroughly. Cut the chicken into bite-size pieces and cook as above. Toss the pasta through the chicken sauce together with 2 cups arugula.

quail, sugar snaps, & baby corn

Serves **2**

Preparation time **10 minutes**, plus marinating

Cooking time **about 12 minutes**

2 **quails**, partly boned

5 oz **sugar snap peas**, halved

5 oz **baby corn**, halved lengthwise

1 **garlic clove**, crushed

1 tablespoon **vegetable oil**

2 teaspoons **sesame oil**

2 teaspoons **light soy sauce**

Marinade

1 small **shallot**, chopped

1 inch **fresh ginger root**, peeled and grated

1 tablespoon **pomegranate syrup**

1 tablespoon **sweet soy sauce**

1 tablespoon **brown rice vinegar**

½ tablespoon **tamarind paste**

1 teaspoon **five spice powder**

Spatchcock the quails, if your butcher has not done so, by removing the backbone, snipping off the wing tips, and flattening the bird with the palm of your hand.

Make the marinade by mixing together all the ingredients in a large bowl. Add the quails and turn to coat, cover, and leave in the refrigerator for at least 8 hours but preferably overnight.

Heat a heavy skillet over a medium heat. Cook the quails for 8–10 minutes, turning once and basting regularly with the marinade. Once the quails are cooked through and sticky, remove them from the pan, cover with foil, and keep warm.

Heat a clean, nonstick skillet over a high heat. Toss the sugar snap peas and baby corn in a bowl with the garlic and vegetable oil and then pour into the skillet. Cook quickly for 2 minutes, moving them occasionally so they don't stick. Return them to the bowl, toss with the sesame oil and soy sauce, and serve immediately, topped with the sticky quail and any juices.

For tofu & pomegranate salad, halve 7 oz tofu horizontally. Make the marinade as above, put the tofu in a nonmetallic dish and cover with the marinade. Cover and refrigerate for at least 30 minutes. Heat a skillet over a high heat and cook the tofu, turning once, for about 2 minutes. Meanwhile, prepare the salad as above, stir through the garlic, vegetable and sesame oils, and soy sauce together with the seeds from a pomegranate. Serve with the cooked tofu.

tuna with tomato & herbs

Serves **2**
Preparation time **15 minutes**
Cooking time **25–35 minutes**

2 fresh **tuna steaks**, each
 about 5 oz
1 large **garlic clove**, cut into
 fine slivers
2 teaspoons lightly ground
 coriander seeds
2 tablespoons finely chopped
 mint, plus extra to serve
2 teaspoons **capers**, drained
salt and **black pepper**

Tomato and herb sauce
2 tablespoons **olive oil**
1 large **garlic clove**, finely
 chopped
½ teaspoon crumbled dried
 red chili (optional)
1 teaspoon dried **oregano**
2 tablespoons roughly
 chopped **mint**
4 tablespoons **dry white wine**
2 large **tomatoes**, skinned,
 seeded, and roughly
 chopped

Use a sharp knife to make small incisions in the tuna steaks. Insert some garlic, coriander seeds, and mint into each opening.

Make the sauce. Heat a little of the oil in a saucepan, add the garlic, chili, oregano, and any coriander seeds remaining from the tuna. Cook, stirring, until the garlic turns golden brown. Add the mint, wine, and tomatoes and cook over a medium heat for 5–10 minutes.

Heat the remaining oil in a small flameproof casserole on the stovetop. Add the tuna and seal on both sides. Pour the sauce over the tuna, season to taste with salt and pepper, and transfer the casserole to a preheated oven, 425°F, and cook for 15–20 minutes.

Sprinkle the baked tuna with a little mint and the capers. Serve with new potatoes and steamed spinach, collard greens, or broccoli.

For tuna pasta bake, cook 6 oz pasta shapes in boiling water according to the instructions on the package. Drain and transfer to an ovenproof dish. Flavor and cook the tuna and make the sauce as above. Flake the tuna and spoon it and the sauce over the pasta. Sprinkle with 4 tablespoons fresh multigrain bread crumbs and 2 tablespoons grated Parmesan cheese. Cook under a preheated hot broiler for 1–2 minutes until golden.

tofu pad thai

Serves **2**
Preparation time **10 minutes**
Cooking time **5 minutes**

2 tablespoons **vegetable oil**
5 oz **tofu**, cut into bite-size
 pieces
2 **garlic cloves**, sliced
pinch of **dried red pepper
 flakes**
bunch of **scallions**, sliced
½ cup **bean sprouts**
5 oz **flat rice noodles**
2 **eggs**, beaten
3 tablespoons **fish sauce
 (nam pla)** (optional)
juice of 1 **lime**
2 tablespoons roasted **salted
 peanuts**, roughly chopped
2 tablespoons chopped
 cilantro

Heat the oil in a wok or skillet. Add the tofu and fry for
2 minutes, then add the garlic, pepper flakes, scallions,
and bean sprouts. Fry for a minute more.

Cook the noodles according to the instructions on the
package. Drain and add to the pan. Heat through, then
stir in the eggs, fish sauce (if using), and lime juice and
continue to cook, stirring, until the egg is cooked. Serve
sprinkled with the peanuts and cilantro.

For shrimp pad thai, cook 5 oz noodles according to
the instructions on the package. Fry the garlic, pepper
flakes, scallions, bean sprouts as above. Stir in the
drained noodles and add 5 oz cooked peeled shrimp
to the pan. Add the beaten eggs, fish sauce, and lime
juice, stirring until the eggs are cooked, and serve
immediately.

scallop, & pancetta linguini

Serves **2**
Preparation time **5 minutes**
Cooking time **10 minutes**

5 oz **linguini**
1 tablespoon **olive oil**
4 oz **pancetta**, chopped
1 **garlic clove**, crushed
1 **red chili**, chopped (optional)
8 **scallops**, halved
1¼ cups **arugula leaves**

Cook the linguini according to the instructions on the package. Drain.

Meanwhile, heat the oil in a skillet. Add the pancetta and cook for a couple of minutes until it is beginning to brown, add the garlic and chili (if using), and fry for a minute more. Add the scallops to the pan and cook for another minute, turning halfway through cooking.

Toss the linguini with the arugula, add the scallops, and serve immediately.

For angler fish pasta, cook 5 oz pasta shapes according to the instructions on the package. Cook the pancetta as above, and add a crushed garlic clove and a seeded and chopped red chili. Cut 7 oz angler fish fillet into cubes and add to the pan, cooking for an additional 2 minutes or until the fish is cooked through. Add the pasta to the pan, stir through to combine with the arugula leaves, and serve.

mediterranean pork casserole

Serves **2**
Preparation time **10 minutes**
Cooking time **1 hour**

1 tablespoon **olive oil**
8 oz **lean pork**, cubed
1 **red onion**, cut into thin
  wedges
1 **garlic clove**, crushed
1 **yellow bell pepper**, cored,
  seeded, and chopped
8 **artichoke hearts**, drained
  and quartered
7 oz can **chopped tomatoes**
1 small glass **red wine**
⅓ cup **black olives**
grated zest of 1 **lemon**
1 **bay leaf**
1 **thyme** sprig, plus extra
  to garnish

Heat the oil in an ovenproof casserole. Add the pork and fry for 2–3 minutes until browned all over. Remove the pork from the casserole with a slotted spoon and set aside.

Add the onion, garlic, and yellow bell pepper to the casserole and fry for 2 minutes. Return the pork to the casserole together with the remaining ingredients.

Bring to a boil, cover, and simmer for about an hour or until the meat is tender. Garnish with thyme and serve accompanied with garlic bread.

For cranberry bean casserole, cook the onion, garlic, yellow bell pepper, artichoke hearts, and tomatoes as above. Rinse and drain 13 oz can of cranberry beans and add to the casserole with the wine, olives, lemon zest, and herbs. Bring to a boil and cook slowly for about 1 hour. Serve garnished with chopped parsley.

duck breast salad with orange

Serves **2**
Preparation time **15 minutes**
Cooking time **15–20 minutes**

2 boneless **duck breasts**
2 handfuls of mixed **arugula and watercress leaves**, chopped
2 **oranges**, peeled and segmented
salt and **black pepper**

Dressing
2 tablespoons **olive oil**
1 tablespoon **balsamic vinegar**
1 **garlic clove**, crushed
pinch of powdered **mustard**
good pinch of **sugar**

Lay the duck breasts, skin side down, on a board, cover with plastic wrap or waxed paper and using a rolling pin, bash them to flatten them slightly. Remove the plastic wrap, turn the breasts over, and score the skin diagonally or in a crisscross pattern with a very sharp knife. Rub the skin all over with salt.

Put the duck breasts, skin side up, on a rack in a roasting pan and cook in a preheated oven, 400°F, for 15–20 minutes or until the duck is brown on the outside but a little pink in the middle.

Meanwhile, cut the skin off the oranges and cut into segments, working over a bowl to catch the juice. Add the orange juice to the ingredients for the dressing, season to taste with salt and pepper, and stir well.

Transfer the cooked duck breasts onto a cutting board and slice them thinly on the diagonal. Put the chopped arugula and watercress leaves in the center of 2 serving plates and arrange the duck slices and orange segments on top.

Beat the dressing and spoon it over the salad.

For duck & noodle salad, cook 2 boneless duck breasts as above and cut into thick slices. Cook 4 oz egg noodles according to the instructions on the package. Drain. In a bowl beat together the juice of 1 orange, 1 teaspoon sesame oil, and 1 teaspoon honey. Combine the noodles with the dressing and stir through 1 tablespoon sesame seeds, 4 oz blanched sugar snap peas, 2 segmented oranges, and 2 sliced scallions. Arrange the duck on the salad and serve.

desserts

ginger peaches & vanilla cream

Serves **2**
Preparation time **10 minutes**
Cooking time **15 minutes**

2 fresh **peaches**, halved and
pitted
1 piece **stem ginger**, finely
chopped
2 tablespoons **ginger syrup**
3 **ginger cookies**, roughly
crushed
2 tablespoons **unsalted
butter**, melted

Cream
4 tablespoons **heavy cream**
seeds of 1 **vanilla bean**
1 tablespoon **confectioners'
sugar**

Put the peaches, cut side, up in an ovenproof dish. Mix
together the ginger, syrup, cookies, and butter and
spoon over the peaches.

Cook in a preheated oven, 400°F, for 12–15 minutes
until bubbling and the peaches are tender.

Whip together the cream with the vanilla seeds and
confectioners' sugar until just stiff and serve with the
peaches.

For almondy baked pears, halve and core 2 fresh
pears. Mix together 1 tablespoon melted butter and
the grated zest and juice of 1 small orange. Cut 1 oz
marzipan into 4 and use the pieces to fill the cavities
of the pears. Drizzle over the butter mixture and bake
in a preheated oven, 400°F, for 12–15 minutes.
Serve with sour cream and a sprinkling of toasted
slivered almonds.

vanilla cheesecakes & rhubarb

Makes **2**

Preparation time **10 minutes**,
plus chilling

Base

3 **oat cookies**, roughly
crushed

1 tablespoon **unsalted butter**,
melted

1 tablespoon toasted
hazelnuts, chopped

Cheesecake

6 tablespoons **cream cheese**

4 tablespoons **mascarpone
cheese**

1 tablespoon **confectioners'
sugar**

few drops of **vanilla extract**

Rhubarb

4 sticks of **rhubarb**, chopped

2 tablespoons **superfine
sugar**

Make the bases. Mix together the cookies, butter, and
hazelnuts and press the mixture into the base of
2 large ramekins or serving dishes. Chill for 10 minutes.

Beat together the cream cheese with the mascarpone,
confectioners' sugar, and vanilla extract and spoon over
the base. Chill for 10 minutes.

Meanwhile, put the rhubarb and sugar in a medium
pan and simmer gently until the rhubarb is tender.
Allow to cool, then spoon over the cheesecake and serve.

For ginger & raspberry cheesecakes, make the
bases with 3 crushed ginger cookies, 1 tablespoon
unsalted butter, and 1 tablespoon chopped hazelnuts.
Make the cheesecake as above and stir through 1 cup
roughly crushed raspberries. Before serving sprinkle
a few more whole raspberries on top together with
1 tablespoon grated semisweet chocolate.

pear pancakes

Serves **2**
Preparation time **10 minutes**
Cooking time **20 minutes**

2 tablespoons **unsalted
  butter**, melted
¼ cup **self-rising flour**
2½ tablespoons **whole-wheat
  self-rising flour**
1 tablespoon **steel-cut oats**
½ tablespoon **superfine
  sugar**
1 **egg**, lightly beaten
⅔ cup **buttermilk**, for thinning
  (optional)
vegetable oil, for brushing
3 **pears**, peeled, cored, and
  chopped
pinch of **cinnamon**
1 tablespoon **water**

Mix together the butter, flours, oats, sugar, egg, and buttermilk to make a smooth batter, adding a little extra milk if the mixture looks very thick.

Brush a nonstick skillet with a little oil and heat. Add a ladleful of batter to the pan and cook for 2 minutes on each side until golden. Remove the pancake from the pan and keep warm. Repeat with the remaining batter mixture to make 6 small pancakes in total.

Meanwhile, put the pears and cinnamon in a small saucepan with the water. Cover and cook gently for 2–3 minutes until just tender. Serve the pancakes with the cooked pears.

For blackberry & almond pancakes, make the pancakes as above. Put 1 cup blackberries in a saucepan and add 1 tablespoon water and 1 tablespoon superfine sugar. Heat, stirring, until softened. Spoon the mixture over the pancakes, sprinkle with 1 tablespoon toasted almonds, and serve.

honey roasted figs

Serves **2**
Preparation time **5 minutes**
Cooking time **20 minutes**

6 ripe fresh **figs**
1 tablespoon **honey**
grated zest and juice of 1
  orange
pinch of **ground cinnamon**
2 tablespoons **sour cream**
1 tablespoon chopped **mint**

Cut a deep cross in each fig and place them in an ovenproof dish.

Mix together the honey, orange zest and juice, and cinnamon and pour over the figs. Cook in a preheated oven, 375°F, for about 20 minutes or until bubbling and the figs are squidgy.

Mix together the sour cream and mint and serve with the figs.

For honey mascarpone figs with raspberries, cut a deep cross in 6 figs and place them in a serving dish. Mix together 2 tablespoons mascarpone cheese with 1 tablespoon honey and spoon the mixture into the figs. Put 1¼ cups raspberries in a small pan with 1 teaspoon confectioners' sugar and cook, stirring, over a low heat until the raspberries are beginning to soften. Serve with the figs.

yogurt with berry coulis

Serves **2**

Preparation time **5 minutes**,
  plus chilling

6 tablespoons **heavy cream**
6 tablespoons **plain yogurt**
¾ cup **blueberries**
¾ cup **raspberries**
3 tablespoons **superfine
  sugar**
2 tablespoons **dark brown
  sugar**

Put the cream and yogurt in a bowl and whip together until just firm.

Put the blueberries and raspberries in a small saucepan. Cook over a low heat for 5–6 minutes until the juices start to ooze. Process with a hand blender or push through a sieve.

Stir the cream mixture into the fruit and spoon into 2 individual ramekins or glasses. Sprinkle with the dark brown sugar and chill in the refrigerator for 15 minutes until the sugar has dissolved on the top. Serve.

For yogurt with tropical fruit coulis, mix together 6 tablespoons each of heavy cream and plain yogurt. Blend together the flesh of 1 ripe mango and 1 passion fruit. Stir through the yogurt mixture and top with dark brown sugar as above. Chill for 15 minutes before serving.

pineapple panettone

Serves **2**
Preparation time **4 minutes**
Cooking time **2–3 minutes**

4 **pineapple rings** in juice,
  drained
4 slices of **panettone**
1 cup **mini marshmallows**
¼ cup **macadamia nuts**,
  crushed
2 tablespoons **vanilla sugar**
confectioners' sugar, to dust

Pat the pineapple rings dry on paper towels and arrange them on 2 slices of panettone. Sprinkle with the marshmallows and crushed macadamia nuts followed by the vanilla sugar. Top with the remaining 2 slices of panettone.

Toast in a sandwich grill for 2–3 minutes or according to the manufacturer's instructions until the bread is golden and the marshmallows are beginning to melt. Slice each sandwich into small rectangles and dust with confectioners' sugar. Serve immediately.

For mango & almond panettone, replace the pineapple rings with 4 slices of mango. Sprinkle with 1 cup mini marshmallows and ½ cup slivered almonds and toast as above.

baked chocolate cheesecake

Serves **2**
Preparation time **10 minutes**,
  plus cooling
Cooking time **45 minutes**

2 tablespoons **unsalted
  butter**, melted
1 cup crushed **ratafia
  cookies**
⅔ cup **cream cheese**
2 tablespoons **superfine
  sugar**
3 tablespoons **mascarpone
  cheese**
2 oz **semisweet chocolate**,
  melted
1 **egg**
1 **egg yolk**

To decorate
sour cream
chocolate shavings

Melt the butter in a saucepan. Add the crushed cookies and mix well. Divide the mixture between two tart pans, 4 inches across, and press down to form the cheesecake bases.

Place the cream cheese, superfine sugar, mascarpone, and chocolate in a small pan and warm over a gentle heat, stirring until the mixture is melted and blended.

Remove from the heat, allow to cool, and then beat in the egg and the yolk.

Divide the chocolate mixture between the two tart pans, place them on a baking sheet and cook in a preheated oven, 350°F, for 45 minutes or until set. Remove from the oven and allow the cheesecakes to cool before transferring them to the refrigerator. Chill until required, then decorate with a dollop of sour cream and chocolate shavings.

For white chocolate & raspberry cheesecake, make the base as above. Mix together the cream cheese, superfine sugar, and mascarpone as above, but using 2 oz melted white chocolate instead of the dark chocolate. Allow to cool, beat in the egg and egg yolk, and stir ½ cup raspberries through the mixture. Bake as above.

italian rice pudding

Serves **2**
Preparation time **10 minutes**,
   plus infusing
Cooking time **25 minutes**

3 tablespoons **raisins**
2 tablespoons **Marsala**
1 **vanilla bean**
1¼ cups **milk**
1–2 tablespoons **superfine
   sugar**
finely grated zest of ½ **orange**,
   plus extra for decorating
¼ teaspoon **ground
   cinnamon**
¼ cup **risotto rice**
3 tablespoons **heavy cream**
toasted slivered **almonds**,
   to decorate

Put the raisins and Marsala in a bowl and allow to soak.

Use the tip of a small, sharp knife to score the vanilla bean lengthwise through to the center. Put it in a heavy saucepan with the milk, bring just to a boil, then remove from the heat and allow to infuse for 20 minutes.

Stir the sugar, orange zest, and cinnamon into the milk and return the pan to the heat. Tip in the rice and cook very gently, stirring frequently, for about 15 minutes until the mixture is thick and creamy and the rice is tender.

Stir in the steeped raisins and cream and heat gently for 2 minutes more. Serve warm, decorated with slivered almonds and grated orange zest.

For crunchy brûlée rice pudding, spoon the cooked rice pudding into 2 ramekins or small, ovenproof dishes. Sprinkle 1 tablespoon Demerara sugar over the top of each and cook under a preheated hot broiler until the sugar has dissolved and is bubbling. Allow to cool until the sugar has hardened, and then serve.

walnut toast & fruit compote

Serves **2**

Preparation time **5 minutes**,
plus infusing

Cooking time **5 minutes**

Compote

1 cup mixed dried **fruit**, such
as apricots, figs, and prunes

²⁄₃ cup **apple juice**

²⁄₃ cup strong **black tea**

1 **star anise**

1 **cinnamon stick**

Toast

1 tablespoon **unsalted butter**

good pinch of **ground
cinnamon**

2 slices of **walnut bread**

1 tablespoon **superfine sugar**

Put the dried fruit, apple juice, tea, star anise, and
cinnamon stick in a small saucepan and bring to a
boil. Remove the pan from the heat and set aside for
20 minutes.

Mix together the butter and cinnamon and spread half
over 1 side of each slice of bread. Put the bread on a
foil-lined baking sheet under a preheated hot broiler
and cook for 1–2 minutes until golden. Repeat with the
other side.

Serve the toast with the cooled compote and a scoop
of vanilla ice cream.

For walnut toast & mixed berries, put 2 cups frozen
mixed berries in a saucepan with 1 tablespoon
confectioners' sugar and, if desired, a drizzle of crème
de cassis. Cook over a medium heat until defrosted
and the juices are oozing. Prepare the toast as above.
Serve the berries on the toasts with ice cream.

cherry clafoutis

Serves **2**
Preparation time **5 minutes**
Cooking time **30 minutes**

1 cup **cherries**, pitted
¾ cup **whole milk**
3 tablespoons **light cream**
few drops of **vanilla extract**
2 **eggs**
¼ cup **superfine sugar**
¼ cup **all-purpose flour**
1 tablespoon roughly chopped
   blanched **almonds**
confectioners' sugar, to dust

Butter a medium ovenproof dish and put the cherries in it. Heat the milk, cream, and vanilla extract in a small pan.

Beat together the eggs and sugar until light and fluffy, then stir in the flour. Gradually stir in the heated milk, then pour this batter mix over the cherries and sprinkle the almonds over the top.

Bake in a preheated oven, 375°F, for 25–30 minutes until golden and puffy. Serve with sour cream, if desired.

For plum clafoutis, halve and pit 4 ripe plums and place them in an ovenproof dish. Make the batter as above, pour it over the plums, and cook in a preheated oven, 375°F, for 25–30 minutes. Serve with ice cream.

chocolate & orange mousse

Serves **2**
Preparation time **10 minutes**,
 plus chilling

3 oz **semisweet chocolate**
grated zest and juice of
 ½ **orange**, plus extra zest
 to decorate
2 tablespoons **heavy cream**
1 **egg**, separated
1 tablespoon **superfine sugar**

Put the chocolate, orange zest and juice, and cream in a small bowl over a pan of gently simmering water and heat gently until the chocolate has melted. Allow to cool, then beat in the egg yolk.

Meanwhile, beat the egg white until it forms soft peaks, add the sugar, and beat until stiff.

Gently fold the egg white into the chocolate mixture, then spoon into glasses or ramekins. Chill for about 1 hour and decorate with orange zest before serving.

For minty choc pots, melt 3 oz chocolate with 6 chocolate mints and 2 tablespoons heavy cream. Continue as above, but before spooning the mixture into 2 serving dishes fold through 4 finely chopped mint and chocolate sticks.

toffee bananas & vanilla cream

Serves **2**
Preparation time **5 minutes**
Cooking time **5 minutes**

2 tablespoons **unsalted butter**
2 tablespoons **dark brown sugar**
2 large **bananas**, sliced
½ cup **heavy cream**
1 teaspoon **rum**

Vanilla cream
4 tablespoons **heavy cream**
few drops of **vanilla extract**

Put the butter and sugar in a nonstick skillet. Heat gently until the sugar has melted. Add the bananas and toss in the sauce for 1–2 minutes until warm and soft. Add the cream and rum and heat through.

Make the vanilla cream by whipping the cream and vanilla extract until just light and beginning to hold its shape. Serve with the bananas and drizzle with toffee sauce, if desired.

For toffee pineapple, melt 2 tablespoons unsalted butter with 2 tablespoons brown sugar in a skillet. Add 2 thick slices of fresh pineapple, skinned and cored, and cook, turning once, for 2–3 minutes. Add 2 tablespoons light cream and 1 teaspoon rum. Serve with vanilla cream or ice cream.

lavender syllabub

Serves **2**

Preparation time **15 minutes**,
  plus infusing

1 tablespoon **superfine sugar**
12 **lavender heads** or a few
  drops lavender cooking
  essence, plus extra lavender
  heads to decorate
6 tablespoons **medium white
  wine**
⅔ cup **heavy cream**

Put the sugar, lavender heads, and wine in a small
saucepan, heat gently until the sugar has dissolved,
then allow to stand for 10 minutes to allow the flavor
to develop.

Strain the mixture, then add the cream and whip until it
forms soft peaks. Transfer to serving glasses and chill.
Serve each syllabub decorated with a lavender head,
if desired.

For orange syllabub, put 1 tablespoon superfine
sugar and the grated zest and juice of 1 orange into a
small saucepan with 6 tablespoons white wine. Cook
gently until the sugar has dissolved, then proceed
as above.

plums in wine

Serves **2**
Preparation time **5 minutes**
Cooking time **10 minutes**

1 ¼ cups **white wine**
½ cup **superfine sugar**
grated zest and juice of
  1 **orange**
1 **star anise**
2 **cardamom pods**
6 fresh **plums**
1 tablespoon chopped
  pistachios

Put the wine, sugar, orange zest and juice, star anise, and cardamom pods in a medium saucepan. Heat gently until the sugar has dissolved.

Add the plums to the wine mixture and simmer for 5–8 minutes or until tender. Remove the plums from the pan and divide between 2 dessert dishes.

Boil the wine mixture until it has reduced to a syrupy consistency. Pour it over the plums and sprinkle with the pistachios. Serve with crème fraîche or ice cream, if desired.

For pears in wine, heat 1 ¼ cups red wine with the sugar, orange zest and juice, star anise, and cardamom pods as above. Peel 2 pears, add them to the saucepan, and simmer 10 minutes. Transfer the pears to 2 dessert dishes and reduce the wine mixture to a syrup. Pour the syrup over the pears and sprinkle with 1 tablespoon slivered, toasted almonds. Serve with cream.

pecans, berries, & ice cream

Serves **2**
Preparation time **20 minutes**
Cooking time **5 minutes**

½ cup **pecan nuts**
2 tablespoons **superfine sugar**
½ tablespoon **unsalted butter**
2 cups mixed **berries**, such as blackberries, raspberries, and strawberries

Vanilla ice cream
1 **vanilla bean**
1¼ cups **heavy cream**
1 tablespoon **superfine sugar**
2 **egg yolks**

Make the ice cream. Split the vanilla bean lengthwise and scrape out the seeds. Put them in a medium saucepan with the cream and the sugar and heat to dissolve the sugar.

Beat the egg yolks in a bowl. Beating continually, pour the cream mixture over the yolks, return to the pan and heat gently, without allowing the mixture to boil, until just thickened. Transfer to a freezerproof container and freeze.

Put the nuts, sugar, and butter in a small saucepan and cook for 1–2 minutes, stirring, until the sugar has caramelized. Remove from the heat stir in the berries, then tip the mixture onto some waxed paper. When it is cold tap with a rolling pin to break into pieces. Serve the ice cream with the pecans and mixed berries.

For caramel pecan ice cream, make the pecan caramel as above. Fold together 1¼ cups fresh custard and 4 tablespoons whipped cream and a few drops vanilla extract. Fold in the pieces of pecan caramel, then transfer to a freezerproof container and freeze until solid.

chocolate & hazelnut meringues

Serves **2**
Preparation time **10 minutes**
Cooking time **1 hour**, plus
  cooling

Meringues
2 **egg whites**
½ cup **superfine sugar**
⅓ cup toasted **hazelnuts**,
  chopped
¼ cup coarsely grated
  semisweet chocolate

Filling
6 tablespoons **whipping
  cream**
1 tablespoon **superfine sugar**

Put the egg whites in a clean bowl and beat until soft peaks form. Keep beating and add the sugar a spoonful at a time. Fold in half of the nuts and half of the chocolate.

Spoon 8 spoonfuls on a lined baking sheet and sprinkle with the remaining nuts. Cook in a preheated oven, 275°F, for about 1 hour. Turn off the oven and leave the meringues in the oven until they are cold.

Whip the cream and sugar to form soft peaks. Melt the remaining chocolate and fold it into the cream to create a marble effect. Use the chocolate cream to sandwich 2 meringues together and serve.

For blueberry & raspberry meringue, use the meringue ingredients above to make 1 large nest. Cook and allow to cool as above. Fill the meringue nest with the cream mixture and top with 1¾ cups fresh mixed blueberries and raspberries. Dust with confectioners' sugar and unsweetened cocoa powder before serving.

summer fruit slush

Serves **2**
Preparation time **5 minutes**

about 2½ cups **summer
   fruits**, such as strawberries,
   raspberries, red currants,
   and blackberries, plus extra
   to decorate
about 5 tablespoons **vanilla
   syrup**, plus extra to serve
   (optional)
crushed ice

Hull the strawberries (if necessary) and blend the
fruit in a food processor or blender until completely
smooth. Remove the seeds by straining the puree
through a nonmetallic strainer into a large pitcher. Stir
in the vanilla syrup.

Fill 2 tall, narrow drinking glasses or sundae glasses
with crushed ice and pour in the vanilla-flavored
fruit mixture.

Pile extra fruits on top of the drinks. Serve with long
spoons and extra syrup, if desired, for stirring in.

For tropical fruit slush, combine about 1 lb mixed
tropical fruits, such as mango, kiwifruit and pineapple.
Continue as above.

index

acknowledgments

Executive Editor: Nicola Hill
Editor: Amy Corbett
Design Manager: Tokiko Morishima
Designer: Nicola Liddiard, Nimbus Design
Photographer: Stephen Conroy
Home Economist: Emma Jane Frost
Props Stylist: Liz Hippisley
Production Controller: Carolin Stransky

Special photography: © Octopus Publishing Group Ltd/Stephen Conroy.
Other photography: © Octopus Publishing Group Ltd/Eleanor Skans 17, 153, 173; /Frank Adam 36, 82, 129, 145, 175, 181, 189; /Gareth Sambridge 52, 55, 95, 99, 205, 215, 233; /Lis Parsons 13, 18, 21, 23, 33, 61, 88, 107, 139; /Stephen Conroy 8; /Will Heap 39, 45, 69, 74; 117, 169, 198.